"Bell's intensely personal memoir is a driven, dangerous coming-of-age story with a heart full of punk love and the self-determined spirit of a girl gone artistically wild."
JONI RODGERS, NEW YORK TIMES BEST SELLING AUTHOR

"Moving and inspirational. Rips the inadequate Band-Aid off childhood wounds and shows that healing is possible. Anyone who's worked with disturbed adolescents will relate to Jessica's story and learn from it. Many children who bear the brunt of 'caring' for parents, are forced into an adult role, and their voices are rarely heard. ... Jessica's self-destructive urges, fuelled by alcoholism and comfort sex, add to the likelihood that she will suffer. The vicious cycle is not easy reading but has an honesty and self-awareness that helps the reader understand why a youngster would behave this way. ... Creativity proves to be a better friend than alcohol or sex, and is also the lifeline which allows the love between mother and daughter to reach an adult understanding, all the more beautiful for its roots in darkness."
JEAN GILL, AUTHOR OF *HOW BLUE IS MY VALLEY*

"Real, raw, and beautifully told. Bell shares an intense tale of overcoming a deep depression that gripped her as a young child, and clung on to her into adulthood, with unrestrained emotional honesty and guts."
SAMANTHA VÉRANT, AUTHOR OF *SEVEN LETTERS FROM PARIS*

"A memoir for anyone who has ever felt alone. A memoir for those who are so hungry for love they'll do anything. A memoir so honest it rips at your heart. This book is what happens when a poet/songwriter/novelist/singer pours her soul onto the page and the angst, pathos, and agony of feeling 'different than' reverberates in our souls."
KAREN WALKER, AUTHOR OF *FOLLOWING THE WHISPERS*

about the author

Before Jessica Bell started writing she was just a young woman with a "useless" Bachelor of Arts degree and a waitressing job.

For information about Jessica and her creative projects, visit, *iamjessicabell.com*.

GO: A Memoir about Binge-drinking, Self-hatred, and Finding Happiness
Copyright © 2021 Jessica Bell
All rights reserved.
Paperback ISBN: 978-1-925965-56-8
ePub ISBN: 978-1-925965-57-5

Previously published in 2017 as
Dear Reflection: I Never Meant to be a Rebel (A Memoir)

No parts of this publication may be reproduced, stored in a retrieval system, or transmitted in any form or by any means, electronic, mechanical, photocopying, recording, or otherwise, without the prior written permission of the copyright owner. This book is sold subject to the condition that it shall not, by way of trade or otherwise, be lent, resold, hired out, or otherwise circulated without the publisher's prior consent in any form of binding or cover other than that in which it is published and without a similar condition including this condition being imposed on the subsequent purchaser. Under no circumstances may any part of this book be photocopied for resale.

Cover design by Jessica Bell
Interior design by Amie McCracken

 A catalogue record for this book is available from the National Library of Australia

JESSICA BELL

GO

A MEMOIR ABOUT DRINKING, SELF-HATRED, AND FINDING HAPPINESS

Vine Leaves Press

table of contents

PART ONE: 1985-1993
13

PART TWO: 1994-1996
69

PART THREE: 1996-1998
107

PART FOUR: 1999-2005
175

PART FIVE: 2005-2016
227

ACKNOWLEDGEMENTS
253

LINKS OF INTEREST
255

A LETTER FROM ERIKA BACH
257

note from the author

I have tried to recreate events to the best of my ability, relying on my own memory. While all the events in this book are true, on some occasions I have been creative with the way they play out due to my inability to recall specific details. I have instead filled these gaps in memory with what I assume would be the most logical and fitting details in relation to the era and circumstances. Names and identifying details of characters other than myself and family members have been changed to protect the privacy of the people involved. Some place names have also been changed. In some cases I have compressed or merged events; in others I have made two or three people into one. Likewise, the conversations in this book are based on my memory alone, and though they are not written verbatim, I have retold them in a way that evokes the feeling and meaning of what was said. In all instances, the essence of the events and dialogue is as accurate as I could make it, from my perspective.

For everyone except myself.

part one
1985-1993

go

If my desire to run were tangible, it would be represented by 2D circles on graph paper. Round and round I'd go, drawing curved lines through empty squares, hoping that one day, they'd be coloured in—hoping that one day, my actions would not be the same actions all over again—repeatedly striking through empty squares to meet their own tails.

When I look at you in the mirror, what do I see? I see 2D circles covering my face. A flattened image of developing wrinkles and stale freckles representing my life—a tug of war between youth and middle-age.

I struggle to shift beyond the glass.

My subconscious forms sound waves in the air behind me. It whispers, "Go."

Go where? Every time I run, I take another step towards nothing but myself.

I needed to pee. It was 1985, and I was four. It would be the first time I remember running from emotional struggle by doing something stupid.

My heart beat in my throat, and I trembled in the darkness of my peach-coloured bedroom at 80 Edwin Street, Heidelberg Heights, in Melbourne, Australia—the red brick house with the crooked mailbox and untamed pink and orange rose bushes I shared with my parents until I turned twenty.

I opened my bedroom door a teeny-tiny crack. The freezing air from the corridor slipped through and gave me goose bumps. I imagined the icy cold floor stinging my feet as I navigated the hall, the kitchen, the glasshouse, past the piano, to get to the toilet, and then slamming the glossy pink door to stop the Heidel Monsters from getting in.

I decided against it and pissed in the corner of my bedroom.

I watched the pee soak into the fibres of the mud-stained ash-grey carpet, then wiped my *chishy* with the corner of a pillow and placed it on top of the smelly puddle. I returned to bed and wrapped myself in my feather down doona, shivering until I warmed.

The next day, when my mother, Erika Bach, and stepfather, Demetri Vlass, were preoccupied with recording their song ideas onto their four-track mixer in the music room, they didn't notice a thing. I realized how much I could get away with without anyone ever knowing how I truly felt.

It was a triumph.

A miracle.

My bedroom door wasn't transparent, and my mother didn't really 'have eyes in the back of her head.' There was no real reason to hide other than my own irrational fear of feeling something that could potentially be a challenge to deal with. But it felt powerful to hide. The thrill of obtaining such privacy would soon develop into a cold, selfish, heartless reflection I believed protected me.

She persuaded me to run.

Her voice grew more authoritative until she became 'another me'—a decision maker who knew 'best.'

She didn't.

I sat on Mum's bed, watching her pack a suitcase for us both. I didn't understand. I admired her thick chestnut perm and the black tears running behind her large-framed prescription glasses. I wanted to jump into the suitcase. It seemed like a good opportunity to play.

go

Mum said, "Say goodbye to Demetri, Juice." Because she was crying, I thought it was Demetri's fault.

I wondered if, when I got older, packing a suitcase would make me cry. I decided no, it was silly. Mum was being silly.

I opened Mum's bedroom door. Demetri squatted in the middle of the corridor that led to the music room, the bathroom, the kitchen, the living room, and my bedroom—and housed a floor-to-ceiling cupboard full of vinyl, pharmaceuticals, and all the bits and pieces no-one ever knows where to put. It was like he was trapped at a crossroads and didn't know which direction to choose.

He sobbed like an injured animal. Strands of black curly hair flattened to his cheeks, hands cupped over his mouth, tears rolling over his knobbly knuckles and crooked Greek nose.

I ran to him, fell into his embrace, kissed him on his stubbly cheek.

"Goodbye," I whispered.

I don't remember feeling sad. I thought it was a strange game. Maybe I knew we weren't really going to leave.

We didn't.

Through the many fights, and broken love between my parents, I would soon understand that choices didn't have to be permanent, nor did anyone have to keep promises if they didn't want to.

That night Mum tucked me into bed, as she always did, stroking my hair and telling me how much she loved me. I felt safe and warm. I always felt safe and warm with Mum—until she said goodnight, and left me alone in my bedroom with the door open a crack so light would stream in.

She would leave the corridor light on until she thought

I fell asleep. Sometimes I hadn't fallen asleep when she turned it off, and the only light entering my room came from the street. The suburban street lights projected a streaked pattern through my horizontal blinds over the wall my bed sat against. With the occasional passing car, the pattern would shift like it was momentarily immersed in water.

When the lights were out, I played doctor with my stuffed toys. One of my favourite toys was one I had made myself: an injection. It was concocted from a long thick sewing needle and scrunched up tissues held together with masking tape. I had taken them from the corridor cupboard. I kept the injection hidden under my bed where everything would go when Mum told me to tidy my room.

I lined up my stuffed toys on my bed so the streaked glow of street lights rippled over their bodies. One by one I gave them 'vaccines.' Each time, right before I stuck the needle in, I'd say, "Now, it's only going to hurt a little bit, okay?"

Loneliness is a powerful feeling.

It mutates inside us, from the moment we take our first breath.

When I started Prep in 1986 at Heidelberg Primary School, I was not quite five as my birthday fell on February 26. Mum took me to my first school fair. I knew she didn't want to go, but she did anyway. I'd asked her to bake, I'm sure of it. She wasn't the baking type, but she made macaroons, or ... something. Maybe she didn't bake at all and I'm remembering something I wished had happened. Though the times she did make macaroons were an absolute treat.

go

People stared at her thick black eyebrows and short black hair. It was now cropped to a sharp bob with a boxed and slightly crooked fringe which she'd cut and styled herself. I liked her black tulle skirt, and the purple and black striped three-quarter length sleeved top with fraying hems, because that was my mum and I knew no different. That was the mother I loved—the mother who'd hold me tightly in her arms until *I* released myself, and who smelled like Myers—a department store in the centre of town with an entire floor devoted to cosmetics and perfume. I could have nuzzled my nose into the nape of her neck all day long to smell that smell. It was comforting and made me feel at home. But I don't think the other mums could see it, or thought she was as pretty as I did. I couldn't understand why they felt the need to stare. Surely my mum should have been the one staring at them in their skin tight blue jeans, bright pink t-shirts, scraggly paper-thin ash-blonde hair, and sheep-coloured moccasins?

Stalls decorated the entire lower-school playground. Mum gave me a few dollars to spend while she went behind the school building to have a smoke—or maybe she went to speak to my teacher. I decided to use the money to buy Mum a present. I'd surprise her, I thought. I was excited. I found a pretty pink hair clip. I think it was in the shape of a bow. When I gave it to her she laughed and hugged me. She said thank you but told me I should keep it. I said, "Why?" She said, "Because your hair is prettier than mine." I later realized that 'prettier' was code for 'longer.' I felt so stupid. Of course she didn't take the hair clip. She didn't have enough hair to clip. I screamed into my pillow that night.

I tossed and turned in my bed, knowing deep down it

was the thought that counted, as Mum had taught me. But I couldn't stop the guilt. I couldn't stop feeling like I had done one of the biggest wrong of wrongs.

You're an idiot. You can't do anything right.

But I thought it was pretty.

You should have just bought something for yourself. You're an idiot ... a stupid stupid stupid idiot!

I grabbed my school bag off my allocated hook and skipped down the school corridor past the principal's office to the exit onto Cape Street in Heidelberg. I think I was in grade one, so it would have been 1987, and I would have been six. Right before I made it to the exit, a fat boy with food smeared all over his face ran into me and slammed me up against the wall. The back of my head rammed into a bag hook and made my teeth bang together. He called me 'stupid.' I stood there and burst into tears, staring into the street as all the other kids filed past me, hardly offering a glance. There were certainly no teachers around to help, and we were far enough away from the principal's office for the incident to be out of his sight.

I waited a few moments to compose myself, then wiped away my tears and walked down hill towards the back entrance of Warringal Shopping Centre, just off Burgundy Road, where Mum was waiting for me to catch the bus home. I decided it would be best to pretend everything was okay as I wanted to appear strong and able to take care of myself, but I hadn't yet mastered the art. My face was flushed and eyes red and Mum saw right through me. She asked me what was wrong. I told her.

Then I saw the boy who pushed me and I pointed him out. I can't remember his name. I think it started with D.

go

Mum walked over to him, grabbed him by his school bag and spun him around to face her. She leaned down so her face was level with his. I couldn't hear what she was saying, but she pointed her finger at him, like she did at me when I misbehaved, and said something that made the boy's face flush. He ran away.

We stepped onto the bus and sat down. "What did you say?" I said.

"I told him if he touched you again I would pull his little penis off."

That made me giggle. Mum was my hero.

But it didn't stop it from happening again.

More and more kids began to tease me and bully me until it became an everyday occurrence. I'm not sure what it was about me.

Was it because Mum looked different?

When we got home, a deep thrumming sound of drums and bass and screeching guitars coming from the music room filled the house. Demetri was recording some guitar for their first Ape the Cry album, And The. It could have been the beginnings of the song 'Don't Expect Too Much.'[1] As Mum slipped into the music room to join Demetri, I dropped my school bag on my bed, made my way into the kitchen, and opened the fridge. I grabbed the red and white carton of Rev milk and took it to the kitchen counter to make myself a Milo, a chocolate drink (with more Milo than milk, of course).

Above the sink was a window that faced the backyard. Hanging on the rose tree outside this window was a rubber tarantula. It always made me giggle to remember the day Demetri and I hung it there. It 'scared the shit

---
[1] You can see a video montage of band shots and clips accompanied by the song 'Don't Expect Too Much' on YouTube here: *bit.ly/ApeTheCry1*.

out of Mum one day when she woke up to make her morning Nescafé. Demetri and I laughed so hard.

I scooped the wet Milo up with a teaspoon and ate it, then drank the milk left in the glass and put it in the sink. I knocked on the door of the music room and opened it enough to poke my head through.

Demetri straddled a Fender electric guitar and Mum clutched a microphone with gaffer tape wrapped around the joint of the cord. Mum reached over Demetri's shoulder and pressed stop on the four-track mixer. I know I must have interrupted them in the middle of a recording, but I was bored.

"Can we play hand ball?" I asked Demetri. Hand ball was what we called hitting a tennis ball against the back wall of the house using our hands as rackets. He looked at Mum for approval.

"He'll be out in half an hour, okay?" Mum said.

I nodded and closed the door behind me.

I went into my bedroom and dragged the drawer of Barbie dolls out from under my bed. I gave one a hair cut to make her look more like Mum.

I immediately regretted it.

What did you do that for?

I shrugged.

She looks horrible.

I know.

I shoved her back in the drawer. I pulled out the other Barbie instead, the brunette that came in the same packet as Ken.

Don't cut her hair too.

I won't.

But I wanted to. I wanted to chop her whole head off.

That same year, while Mum and Demetri spent a

weekend in a professional studio recording their forthcoming *And The* album, they sent me to stay with my biological father, Tony, a high school Maths and Science teacher, and his wife, Margaret, who was a kindergarten teacher.

Tony and Margaret lived in a tiny town house in Brunswick with a bright red kitchen counter and cupboards. Despite the house being spotless, every few hours the counter would be covered in ants. Margaret would get flustered by it, but I just thought it was funny and interesting to watch them in action. Where were they all going? And what for?

"Right!" Margaret clapped her hands together after cleaning away the ants for the third time that day. "What do you want to do?" She straightened her floral skirt with her hands and flicked her shoulder length brown hair out of her eyes.

I shrugged and looked at the cat meowing outside the fly screen. I thought about going into the backyard and dragging around a piece of string for it to try and catch.

"I know ..." Margaret opened a cupboard full of canned and packet goods from the supermarket. She took them all out and lined them up on the counter. She pulled a notepad and pen out of a drawer and a handful of coins from her handbag.

She set me up a shop.

"You be the sales assistant and I'll be the customer." She picked up a bar stool and brought it around for me to sit on. She left the room, and then came back in holding her handbag. She approached the counter and said, "Could I have a can of tuna and a can of tomatoes, please?"

I nodded and said, "Here you are," handing her a can of tuna and a can of tomatoes.

"How much does that come to?" Margaret cocked her head to the side.

I was stuck. I had no idea how much it came to so I just made something up.

"Two dollars, thanks."

Margaret handed me a five dollar note from her wallet and asked for change.

I gave her change from the handful of coins she'd provided me with. It wasn't correct, but Margaret helped me fix it.

"Thank you very much. Have a nice day." Margaret smiled.

I said, "Thank you. Have a nice day too."

Then Margaret sent Tony in to do the same thing. He walked up to the counter, and pushed his glasses up his nose, sniffed, and scratched his head of short, curly, mousy brown hair.

"Um, I'll take this," he said, sliding a packet of water crackers towards me. "How much do I owe ya?"

I was thrilled. It was so fun! And every time I visited them, I'd ask to play shop. I often wonder whether I drove them nuts, insisting they come to buy things over and over pretending to be different people each time. I would scribble gibberish on my notepad as though I was calculating their charge. And I would always be the shop assistant, and never the customer. It made me feel grown up and not at all like I was playing a game. The best part was that I wasn't playing on my own.

Mum has told me that Demetri played with me a lot. But I can't remember many of those moments. I remember hand ball, I remember *asking* him to play with me, regardless of what the game was, I remember games *happened*. But the feelings that came with the playing have vanished. Now, I only remember him saying "Not now."

The luxury of playing shop with Tony and Margaret only occurred a couple of times a month, if that, and it wasn't long before I learnt to enjoy playing alone. I despised school, so I would often pretend I was sick. Of course, Mum believed me for a little while and let me stay home, until she realised I was always sick on Wednesdays when I had Trolley Maths.

As the years passed and I learnt to read and write, I would be sick on other days of the week too. I'm pretty sure Mum knew I was faking, but she also knew I struggled with bullies and so often cut me some slack.

On sick days I'd write up my own personal TV guide using the *Green Guide* from *The Age*, a national newspaper, and sit in bed all day watching my favourite shows on my tiny second-hand black-and-white television set whose antenna needed at least fifteen minutes of jigging before it gained a reception void of white noise.

To this day, I can't live without my alone time watching my favourite TV shows. And it's never quite the same if I have company. If I have company, sometimes I'd rather not watch anything at all.

I lay awake in a pair of pink flannel pyjamas, on a springy fold-out bed, in the middle of a cold empty room at my babysitter's house. The odour of soya milk, Marmite, and vegetarian sausage lived in the carpets and curtains, encompassing the entire house in its stink. Dried pig skins for his African drums were scattered around his house, along with maracas, and netting, and beads.

I closed my eyes and an image of my babysitter chewing

on the pig skins flashed before my eyes. If I went to sleep, I was sure to have a nightmare.

I burst into tears and pulled the layers of thin woollen blankets and patch quilts over my head. Even the bedding smelled like carcass to me. I shivered and cried and prayed for Mum and Demetri to come and pick me up before sunrise, like they often did after a gig if it didn't run too late.

It seemed like I'd been crying for hours when I heard the front door open and Demetri's light footsteps. I wiped my eyes with the covers, rolled over, and pretended to be asleep. He tiptoed inside and scooped me up in his arms. I reminded myself to fall limp in his arms so he didn't notice I was awake.

Demetri whispered, "Hello sweetheart." I made a little groaning sound to make the act more realistic, wrapped my arms around his bony shoulders, and nestled my face into the nape of his neck. The smell of smoke and beer laced his shirt and thick black curls, but that was comforting to me. This smell was a sign I was going home.

With me propped up in Demetri's left arm, and my overnight bag hooked over his right wrist, he walked me to our dark blue VW Beetle. Mum stood outside on the nature strip, holding the passenger door open. I still maintained the fake sleeping, but I opened my eyes a crack and saw Mum's black suede leather boots with square toes and her fishnet stockings.

"How ya wanna do this?" Demetri whispered. On this night, an amplifier was positioned on the front passenger seat, and their tall and lanky Italian bass player was sitting in the back. And as a VW Beetle is only a two door vehicle, the car was popping at the seams.

"Let me get in first," Mum said. The bass player got

go

out of the car via the driver's side, then Mum got in and shuffled over behind the passenger seat. Demetri gently transferred me into the back seat, and Mum lifted me onto her lap and sat me on her left side so I could lean my head against the window. She propped my head up with the little red pillow decorated with white flowers I took everywhere with me. She pulled an orange woollen blanket up around my face to protect me from the cold, kissed my head, and breathed in deep as her lips touched my hair.

"I love you," she whispered. "So so so *so* much."

I smiled, consumed by her perfume and powder smell. *Home*.

The bass player and Demetri re-entered the car, and we chugged off.

My head vibrated against the stiff black leather lining of the back seat, the car rumbling like a lawn mower along some road in St. Kilda at two or three in the morning. The windows fogged up from everyone's breath.

The bass player was squashed in a foetal position against the window along with some other music equipment. The car smelled of gaffer tape. I remember Demetri being proud of how much stuff he could squeeze into the VW Beetle. I knew Mum disliked it, but she didn't often complain. It's all they could afford. It wasn't until adulthood that I realized just how hard my parents worked to support me as much as their music. The love they put into their music, they would give me in equal measure. For years we owned one small electric radiator to warm the whole house during winter. Most of the time, that radiator was in my bedroom, and the one hot water bottle we owned would always grace my sheets.

The warmth of my mother's body soothed the experience at the babysitter's as we headed home. But just as

I drifted off, Mum woke me. For a moment, I thought we had pulled into our driveway. Relief swelled through my body, and I forced myself to open my eyes so I could walk inside on my own. I could soon snuggle up in my feather-down doona and cuddle my stuffed toys.

"Jessica, wake up. Sit up. Smile." Mum shook me a bit and pulled the blanket down so the cop looking into the car via Demetri's window could see my face. Mum smiled at the cop. The cop said something in a deep Australian twang.

"Look—" Mum started to cry. "Do you think if we had the money, we'd drive in a piece of shit like this?"

My parents got pulled over that night because there was too much stuff in the car and it was blocking Demetri's rear view. The fine would have no doubt eaten their entire night's earnings. I recall a conversation about selling a guitar ... or dipping into the 'bread and milk jar'—a jar in a kitchen cupboard that Mum and Demetri would throw coins into and use for basic everyday groceries (and I think sometimes fish and chips, Tatts-Lotto, and the occasional $1 Scratchies from the newsagent's we'd never win.)

I don't know.

If I'd have smiled and charmed the copper, could I have helped prevent that fine?

I spent two hours of after-school care one day locked in a toilet cubicle by choice. It was my second year at school, so I was six, but still terrified of being ridiculed by classmates and scolded by Mrs Wallace, a teacher with a temper who looked like a cross between Queen Elizabeth and Dame Edna Everage.

go

I bawled my eyes out, staring at the watery shit in my knickers and running down my inner thighs.[2] I couldn't move. I had nothing to change into, and no-one to come to my rescue.

I was in after-school care that day because Mum and Demetri were at the recording studio, so a teacher wouldn't have even been able to call home to get me a change of clothes.

I panicked. I cried. I gasped frantically for air when the thought flashed through my mind that no-one would find me before they closed the school and locked me in the toilets until the next morning.

Why did you run away? Why didn't you just tell Mrs Wallace in the playground?

Because I didn't want the other kids to see!

But now you're stuck in here. That was stupid. What are you going to do?

I don't know. I don't know what to do. I don't know what to do!

You're an idiot. You're stupid. Stupid, stupid, stupid!

I wailed and wailed, holding my yellow-and-white striped Miki House Club dress away from my legs—my saturated knickers still hooked around my ankles. I was so afraid of stepping out of the cubicle in case another kid came in. I had to get cleaned up. But how? I couldn't possibly go outside without a pair of knickers on. Everyone would see my *chishy* as my dress was short.

Call for help.

I don't want to.

There's no other way.

But they'll see me, and they'll laugh at me.

---

[2] If you've read my novella, *The Book*, you will recognize this incident, as I used it as inspiration for the story.

Do you want to be locked in here all night?
No.
Then stop being such a wuss and call for help!

"Help!" I cried at the top of my lungs. Only once. But no-one came for what seemed like hours. The shit on my legs was now beginning to dry and go crusty, and the stench was getting stronger and stronger. The sounds of laughter and screaming kids and bouncing balls wafted in ... and then footsteps.

Don't be scared.

I stayed silent.

What are you doing? Say something.

I couldn't. I was tongue-tied with fear.

Say something!

"Jessica?"

I held my breath.

"Jessica, are you in here?"

I let out a soft sob. I tried to hold it in, I really did, but it escaped without my permission.

Mrs Wallace knocked on my cubicle door. "Can I come in?"

"Um–I–I pooed my pants."

A moment of silence.

"Hold on dear, I'll be back in a jiffy."

A couple of minutes later Mrs Wallace returned with the lost property box and found me a pair of white underpants with blue trucks on them. She locked the main entrance to the toilets and led me to the sink to clean me up. She wrapped my underpants in a paper towel and threw them in the bin below the dispenser.

"You won't be needing those again." Mrs Wallace smiled and knelt down to my level. "Why didn't you say anything?"

I looked at my reflection in Mrs Wallace's glasses.

go

Because I'm an idiot and I'm stupid.

I shrugged and looked at my feet.

"Never mind. If there's a next time, there's nothing to be afraid of dear. You just come and tell me and we'll sort it out."

She took my hand and led me outside. "You'll be pleased to know that your dad is here to pick you up."

She took me to the Beetle, but didn't mention the accident. I assume she thought it best for me to tell Demetri myself. After seeing my flushed face and puffy eyes, he asked if I was okay, but I didn't answer.

I got in the car and sat in silence all the way to the studio where I would be placed in a corner with Derwent colouring pencils and paper, and a blanket and pillow, in case I wanted to sleep. I kept repeating in my head, *You're an idiot. You're stupid. You're an idiot. You're stupid.*

I was scared of being hated even more than I thought I already was. But was I? Were kids just being kids? Was I an easy target because I was quiet and reserved and blonde and freckled and small? Again, I had run from the potential of feeling something unpleasant. But for years to come, every time I'd run, I'd end up right where I started—confronting my own reflection.

That day in the toilet cubicle, my reflection started to demean me on a regular basis.

And it would only get worse.

It was a Saturday afternoon in 1988, I was seven, and the Ape The Cry *And The* album was in mid production. Mum stood at the kitchen table, eyes squinted with a cigarette hanging from her mouth, putting together the mock-up of the album cover. Her hair was now short and platinum blond, eyebrows still thick and drawn on with a dark brown pencil. Her grey-blue eyes were accentuated with liquid eyeliner that smelled of cleaning fluid, and her lips were outlined with a deep red lip pencil to make them look bigger. She wore a cream-coloured dress with big red tulips on it which she'd made herself from old curtains. She'd grunged it up with a thick black elastic belt, black stockings, the same pair of black suede square-toed boots she always wore, and mismatched clip-on earrings.

Mum made me a cold Milo and a peanut butter sandwich. I sat at the kitchen table and watched her work. The whole design was on a big piece of white cardboard with layers of semi-transparent graph paper stuck to it. Each layer of graph paper had different parts of the whole image on it, just like we use layers in Photoshop nowadays. In the margins were little colour swatches, which she had drawn on manually. I watched as she rubbed on some lettering with Letraset Transfers.

"What do you think, Juice?" Mum butted her cigarette out into a clay ashtray I'd made her at school.

I didn't know what to say. It was only black, white and—what I thought was horrible at the time—mustard yellow.

"Why can't you add more colours?"

"Because it costs more money to add more than one colour."

I didn't understand why, but I nodded anyway. Demetri walked in with an exhausted groan after working his half-day Saturday shift at the fruit shop in Balwyn Heights. He approached the table and raised his eyebrows. "Looks good."

"Did you get paid?" Mum said.

go

Without a word, Demetri pulled a wad of cash from the back pocket of his dirty black jeans and handed it to Mum. She smiled at me, lit another cigarette, dropped a few twenty cent pieces on the table, and pushed them towards me.

"That's for a bag of lollies."

My entire mood lifted and I propped myself up on my knees on the kitchen chair. "Can I go now?"

"The milk bar's closed now. Tomorrow morning."

I picked up the coins and cradled them in my palm like a prize.

Mum moved the album cover mock-up to the side and started counting the week's money into four different piles.

"Bills. Food. Band. Backyard," she said, and handed the last pile to Demetri. He knew what to do with it. He buried the cash in the backyard where they had a stash stored in an Arnott's Scotch Finger Biscuits tin in a hole in the middle of the lawn. That was our Greece money.

Every three or four years we would go to Greece and stay with Demetri's parents on a little island called Ithaca. Mum saved scrupulously for these trips and my parents would go without luxuries for years to make them happen. They didn't have to save much in those days, though, because the exchange rate from Australian Dollars to the Drachma back then was so good we were able to live like royalty there.

When Demetri came back in, Mum told him to have a shower and get ready. The party guests would start arriving soon.

I spent the next couple of hours helping Mum and Demetri set things up. While Demetri spent the good part of an hour trying to hook up speakers in the backyard through the window of the music room, I helped

Mum prepare a few plates of cheese, cabana and water crackers (while popping bits of cabana into my mouth whenever she wasn't looking). I'm sure there was other food too, but my recollection of the prank gifts she'd made have completely dominated my memory of this day.

I didn't see them during the lead-up, but once all Mum's music industry guests had congregated in the backyard, and downed a couple of beers, Mum came prancing out wearing white balloons taped to a bra with big black nipples drawn on them. She also held a carrot with a condom on it and gave it to her back-up singer. There were multiple other prank gifts in the box but I can't recall what they were.

I do, however, remember the laughter.

I remember the dancing.

I remember thriving on the attention from all the adults there, and despite the loneliness that crept up on me when my parents were too busy to play, I felt a warm sense of belonging and love.

I couldn't understand why I had such a hard time connecting with other kids at school, but when it came to being around adults, I felt right at home. Was the difference I felt on the inside showing on the outside too?

No, you were a wuss.
But I was just a child.
You hated yourself already.
How could I have?
It started a lot earlier than you think.
Why?
Because the world is suffocating and demanding.
The world is what we make it.
Yes. And you made it like that.

That same year Tony and Margaret had a little girl named Allison. A couple of years later they gave me a brother too, and named him after Tony's father, Geoffrey.

I had siblings—something I had never dreamed of.

For some reason, the idea of Mum having another baby seemed as far-fetched as time travel. To me, Mum wasn't a normal person that did normal things. She was not capable of having another child because she was one of the cool people. (In my mind cool people didn't have kids and I was an accident.) I believed Mum's buttons had been switched off and it was the desire of the universe to keep her the same and never change. But maybe I didn't want her to have a child. Maybe I liked being alone and able to fight for her attention without the competition of another kid's fight for it too. It was hard enough without siblings getting Mum to play. In fact, I can't recall ever playing games with Mum. Demetri was apparently the go-to for games, and Mum was the go-to for hugs and discipline. I guess I had accepted this without a second thought. That was the way it was, and it was normal.

A few weeks after Allison's birth, I visited Tony and Margaret.

Margaret stood in the doorway with a smile that reached Hollywood and back, holding Allison in her arms. Tony sat me on the couch, surrounded me with cushions for the big introduction, and told me to hold my arms 'like so.' He demonstrated a cradle. I did what he said, my insides fluttering with nerves. Margaret handed Allison to Tony, and Tony gently rested her in my embrace.

Allison's tiny head rested on my left upper arm, and I rested my left arm on a big cushion so I couldn't feel her weight. I kissed her forehead and her delicate skin was silk on my lips. I remember wondering how she was so light, not comprehending the physics of the whole thing.

And I remember how light *I* felt, sitting in silence laced with a faint gurgle coming from Allison's miniature rose-pink mouth. I held a *whole* human being in my arms. *I* was hugging a child. I was not the one *being* hugged. I wanted to take her home. I wanted to protect her and play with her. I wanted her to love me.

But then her weight started taking its toll.

I winced and tried to adjust my position. Tony and Margaret noticed my discomfort and took her back.

That was fun, I thought. *Now how am I going to draw the attention back to me?*

Though 1988 was the last year *Young Talent Time* aired, we didn't know the show was going to be cancelled. Mum would let me watch it every Friday night at 7:30 p.m. I loved the show so much I wanted to be in it. Though I had never tried to sing properly before, I was convinced that all I had to do was open my mouth and the right notes would come out. After all, that's exactly what all the other kids on the show did, and I had a Mum who did it too. Why couldn't I?

"Can I go on it?" I said, pushing feta cheese omelette and salad around my plate with my fork.

"What would you do?" Mum asked, and glanced at Demetri with a smile. He smiled in response and looked at me with interest, but didn't say anything.

I shrugged and put a bit of omelette in my mouth. Though we weren't big TV watchers in general—except on Friday nights when *Rage* played music videos all through the night and into Saturday morning—we often ate dinner in front of the TV if there was 'something good on.' My parents would sit on the off-white two-seater couch, and I sat on the arm chair that looked like it had been attacked by a carpet from an antique store. I think eating dinner in front of the TV was a treat for my parents too. To be able to sit and enjoy a meal in front of the box, after a long week straddling the line between normal parenthood and the passionate drive to become famous, must have been their only way to recharge their batteries.

"I can sing," I said, after a moment of reflection. But I was unsure. All I wanted, really, was to wear an amazing costume—like the sparkly red one I borrowed from a neighbour's daughter who did calisthenics which I insisted on wearing in Ape the Cry's 'Swim'[3] video clip. I daydreamed of people clapping and adoring me like everyone else on the show.

Mum gathered the last of her salad into a pile on her plate and attempted to scoop it up with her fork. She didn't manage and placed her plate on the coffee table.

"What would you sing?"

"'River?'"

Mum had played Joni Mitchell to me since I was in her womb. And I loved her.

"Okay. Show me how you'd sing it."

"Now?"

"Yes. Let's go into the kitchen, and you can perform for me as if you were on TV. If you're good, I'll get you on the show."

My stomach bubbled with excitement.

I took our plates into the kitchen and left them in the sink. Mum entered a moment later with a cassette player and a tape of Joni's album *Blue*. She pulled out the plug

---

[3] You can watch the 'Swim' video clip here: *bit.ly/ApeTheCry2*. I appear right at the end. You'll notice the clip is in black and white and my costume not visible. Something I'm sure my mother was aware of, as there is no way she'd have let me wear something like that.

of the kettle, replaced it with the cassette player, and inserted the tape. She fast forwarded to track 8—'River'—after a few rounds of pressing the buttons backwards and forwards to reach the right spot.

"Okay. Just sing when she sings," she said, and stepped backwards against the kitchen wall to give me space.

I stood like a statue in front of the canary yellow kitchen cupboards and sung completely off-key, stumbling over Joni's faultless lyrics and melody. Even though the song was clear in my head, it didn't come out of my mouth the way I had hoped.

"Nope—" Mum shook her head. "Sorry."

What? That was it? I'd hardly got through one verse.

"Wait, let me try again?"

"No, Juice, you need practice. When you're a bit older, and can sing, you can go on *Young Talent Time*."

Mum turned the cassette player off and went back into the living room. Feeling rejected and worthless, I retreated to my bedroom and sulked the night away.

You're an idiot. You can't do anything.

Leave me alone!

But what seemed like a big blow to my self-esteem at the time, was actually a huge favour. Mum saved me from being embarrassed in front of the entire country. Perhaps she could have cushioned the truth, let me know in a gentler way. But my mother wasn't like that. She's not like that now, either. There's no beating around the bush with her, and it's something I've come to appreciate and respect.

Because I know when I need her honest opinion, I'm going to get one.

I can trust her.

And trust ... is everything.

go

♦

I sat on the maroon floral-patterned rug in the living room of Mum's back-up singer's townhouse eating cheese Twisties from a blue-glazed ceramic bowl. Her name was Melanie, and I adored her. She was like the big sister I never had. She used to call me Bessie, I imagine because it rhymed with Jessie and sounded cuter.[4]

I listened to Mum, Melanie, and Melanie's housemate/band groupie, talk business. I comprehended nothing except that they suddenly had a lot of lesbian fans and how exciting it was being recognized in the street. Of course, I didn't understand what 'lesbian' meant at that age and thought it had something to do with not eating meat. The connection between music and diet baffled me, but I chose to stay quiet—especially since the last band get-together when I embarrassed myself. They were playing a party game which required everyone to name as many countries or cities starting with a certain letter of the alphabet. When we'd reached M, the bass player, lying casually on his side on the floor, head propped up on his elbow, named Mississippi. I said, "There's a country called Mrs Hippie?"

Everyone laughed. My stomach clenched, and *she* said, once again ...

You're an idiot. Stupid, stupid, stupid!

"I want to go to bed." I blushed and blocked my tears by holding my breath.

Mum put me into the bass player's bedroom and I pretended everything was just fine until she left.

I drenched his wife's pillow.

So, on this evening at Melanie's house, I sat quietly, munching on junk food, keeping my gob shut, as they chatted and gossiped over the latest Crowded House album, *Temple of Low Men*, which was playing in the background.

Then Mum's whole body went stiff. She stopped talking, closed her eyes, and clenched her jaw. Melanie and her housemate continued chatting and laughing about something until they noticed Mum's behaviour.

Still cradling the bowl of Twisties in my lap, I stopped chewing and stared at Mum.

My stomach sank and my heart thumped in my ears. I'd never seen her like this before.

"Erika, are you okay?" Melanie asked, resting her hand on Mum's knee.

Mum opened her eyes and shook her head. "I can't move. I think my back's gone out."

"Shit," Melanie said, standing up. Her housemate stood up too. I followed suit in silence, leaving the bowl of Twisties on the floor. We hovered over Mum like she was a dying bird.

"Hop over a bit, Bess," Melanie said. "We need to make some room for your Mum."

I moved over and Melanie and her housemate shifted the coffee table and pushed an arm chair further into the open plan kitchen.

"How are you going to do this?" Melanie directed the question at Mum, and then glanced at her housemate. "We need to lie her flat on her back."

"Let's just do it," Mum said, wincing and holding her breath, her eyes focussed on her knees.

Melanie and her housemate helped lower Mum to the floor and propped her head up on the flattest cushion Melanie could find. As Mum moved, she made a lengthened sound that resembled a cross between a yelp and a groan.

go

I sat watching at a distance as Melanie and her housemate kneeled by Mum's side asking what she felt and where. I can't remember what she said. I can't even remember how we got home that night, or how long it took for her to recover, but Mum began to have many more back spasms after this.

She was soon falsely diagnosed with osteoarthritis by an ignorant doctor. The doctor prescribed her Brufen—anti-inflammatory pills that were bright pink and looked like Smarties and came in a brown glass bottle—and Valium—a benzodiazepine used to treat anxiety disorders, alcohol withdrawal symptoms, or muscle spasms. In the 50s and 60s Valium was used to relax 'uptight' women when they were having a bad day. Doctors flippantly prescribed it before they realized how badly it could destroy a person's nervous system when taken for long periods of time. The habit to prescribe such drugs still hadn't completely subsided in the 80s.

Mum didn't have osteoarthritis, nor were her muscle spasms due to any specific condition other than years of thinking that popping a pill here and there to relax wouldn't do any harm. It would take her almost ten years to learn that the back spasms were a side effect of over-the-counter drugs in the first place, and her rare paradoxical reaction to sedatives and muscle relaxants.

And thus Mum's drug-dependent existence began.

Mum lay flat on her back in bed, dealing with another back spasm a few weeks leading up to my eighth birthday. She didn't make a big deal about it then, told me not to worry, to go and play with the neighbour's kids.

I could do whatever I wanted. I had a free and unrestricted childhood—born on the cusp of an era when parents could still let their kids ride bicycles around the block on their own, without worrying about abduction.

But what I wanted never seemed to be on the table—Mum's undivided attention—so I would often spend time on my own, in my own world.

In the suffocating heat of February 1989, I squatted below the apricot tree in the middle of our driveway. It was giving birth to rotting fruit in the twilight, staining the cracked concrete with its syrupy-sweet fermenting flesh.

I picked up a twig lying conveniently by my right leg. My knee dug into my chest. I watched as a group of ants fled the area, and wished they would stay.

"I won't hurt you," I whispered.

I'd recently learnt in school how ants spend the summer collecting food for winter, so I decided to break up some apricot with my twig to make it easier for them to transport it to their home. Their queen would be proud of them, and I would have played a small part in their success. I liked the idea of the anonymity, even though, at that age, I would not have been able to give it a name.

"You're welcome," I whispered, as I stabbed a piece of apricot until there were some pieces small enough for the ants to carry.

I waited. Stared. Still squatting. Long enough, still enough, for the ants to trickle back.

One ant took advantage of my help.

I smiled and whispered, "You can do it," as it navigated the cracked concrete with a tiny piece of apricot on its back. It stopped at the edge of a crack about the width of its entire body. I screwed up my mouth in thought, picked up a fallen leaf, and carefully rested it over the crack. The ant turned around and started off in the opposite direction.

go

No, no, no!
You can't do anything right. You're an idiot. Stupid!

Saliva accumulated at the back of my throat the way it did before I was about to cry. I swayed left and right. Sweat trickling between my thighs and lower torso.

Then I heard the VW Beetle—propellers underwater. Demetri chugged into the driveway. I stood to let him pass, stepped backward onto the red-tiled porch steps, and watched him murder the ants.

"Hi Jessie!" He smiled and said something else I paid no attention to as he got out of the car and walked indoors.

I stared at the tyres. Anger and sadness and helplessness coated every organ in my body. Nothing was worth the effort, I decided.

What's the point?
There is none. We just end up hurting.
Or alone. Or dead.

When the dark blue VW Beetle broke down for the last time in 1990, my parents bought another. A white one. Being a year away from double digits and grown out of my everything-needs-to-be-sparkly phase, I didn't like the white one. Dark blue suited us more. It was mysterious, more attractive, and unique. It had a gothic rock edge that blended in with my parents' look. It also matched the migraines I'd get whenever travelling in it for long periods of time, and the stopping on the side of the highway to throw up from the pain. Getting a migraine in a white VW Beetle didn't seem right. It was too pure and friendly. In a white Beetle, my parents needed to look like *The Brady Bunch*, not *The Addams Family*. And at fifteen, when I learnt to drive in the white Beetle, it almost drove me off the edge of the Northland parking lot into Darebin Creek. I didn't think the white Beetle liked my parents much either. It always broke down in the middle of busy roads and was the catalyst of many an argument between Mum and Demetri.

"We can't afford to break down again," she'd say with pursed lips, when we'd get in the car. "What if I have a back spasm in the middle of Punt Road you fucking idiot. I don't feel safe. Fix it."

I didn't blame her for feeling unsafe. But the self-medicating affected her moods, causing her to belittle Demetri and me for all sorts of unfounded reasons.

Even though the white Beetle caused my Mum to worry, I didn't care about it much. I liked it when we broke down. To be in a state of suspended animation, meant I didn't have to *feel* anything, or *be* anything. When we broke down, I felt the world had stopped just for me, and I bathed in the luxury of delay. Delay meant I didn't have to get told off for not cleaning my room, or listen to Mum scream at me and run her arm across my bookshelves smashing my collection of porcelain ornaments and snow balls onto the floor.

"Now clean it up!" she'd scream. Her face never turned red. It turned white. On reflection, that was probably because she was in pain. I didn't know it at the time—and neither did Mum—but those were the beginning of her drug-induced rages.

Of course, at nine years old, all I understood what that my mother was turning into a pure monster who hated my guts.

I hate her.
We'll get her back.
How?

Silence. She hates it when you don't respond.

Mum often accused me of being lazy. But that wasn't it—not entirely. Being left alone meant I could float aimlessly in my own world. I desperately wanted to be an adult—what kid doesn't?—because I would be able to lock myself in my bedroom day and night without anyone looking over my shoulder and telling me what to do. Or was it because I could be away from school where no-one, including my reflection, bullied me, away from a reality where I'd be asked to wash the dishes, or rake the plane tree leaves off the front lawn, or brush my teeth, when I really really *really* didn't want to?

Maybe I *was* lazy.

But maybe that laziness was the first sign of depression.

For about a decade, Demetri kept the blue Beetle in the backyard for 'spare parts.' He kept everything that Mum wanted to throw away for parts. Our red brick garage with the heavy iron door was filled to the brim with cardboard boxes, mechanical bits and pieces, magazines, books and vinyl records from the 70s, splintered pieces of old furniture, and nuts and bolts in jam jars. He couldn't bring himself to throw anything away—even when he discovered he couldn't use them for anything.

He couldn't use the blue Beetle parts for the white Beetle because it was a different model. Whenever something needed replacing in the white Beetle, the blue Beetle bits never fit. He still kept the blue Beetle for 'spare parts.'

Everything in the garage sat collecting dust like bottled memories.

Knowing Demetri as an adult now, I know he has great difficulty in expressing his feelings. He seems to bottle them up to the point where Mum and I see complete blankness. When he does speak, it's either about computers, music, or politics: dinner party conversation. As a kid, I thought his silence meant life was good. If you didn't complain about something, there was nothing to complain about, right? But now I can see deeper. I don't know *what exactly* is deeper, but I'm certain he is dealing with some personal demons. A musician's fate, perhaps?

I believe Demetri liked it when the car broke down, too. Looking back, I feel Demetri buried his demons in the clutter of that garage. The car was also something he could try to fix because he couldn't fix whatever was going on deep inside. And just like the spare parts that didn't fit anywhere, I don't think he could figure out where his feelings fit either. Somehow, despite us not being blood relatives, I believe I inherited his ability to make silence a runaway cave.

Demetri showed me how to hide.

And the blue Beetle showed me a way to hide in plain sight.

Because my parents were creative, they encouraged me to be creative too—except by drawing on my bedroom walls. So one spring weekend in 1990, with our wild jasmine bushes in full bloom, and the huge pile of wood chipping dumped in the middle of our lawn filling our backyard with its masculine scent (it was for one of Mum's totally random and uncharacteristic landscaping ideas which was probably brought on by her increasing anxiety that our garden looked like a garbage tip and the neighbours would think ill of us), I had the idea to clothe the blue Beetle in watercolour graffiti. Of course, I got permission first, and because the body of the vehicle wasn't going to be used for anything, I was allowed to.

But what had initially been a simple fun leisure

activity, turned into something I could never again live without: uninhibited creativity and me-time.

The voice in my head had hushed.

For a short while, I wasn't dreading going to school or feeling sorry for myself, or thinking about the next time Mum would tell me off for not cleaning my room.

The notion that one could be passionate about something and make a living off it, of course, had not yet been considered. I was too young to even understand what a job really meant. But I did understand one thing: nothing in the world mattered except being in the backyard, smelling the woodchips and jasmine, enjoying the warm spring sun, and painting watercolour flowers and rainbows on the dark blue Beetle—a juxtaposition of my life.

I'd found a place I could run to.

Without anyone noticing I'd gone.

By some miracle, when I'd turned ten in 1991, I made a friend. In fact, I called her my best friend then, but maybe that was just the way I felt about her.

Her name was Linda Rollins. Her long silky ginger hair that glistened in the sunlight, accentuated her green eyes, and complemented her aesthetically arranged freckles and smooth skin. She stood tall and poked out her chest as if she already had breasts to flaunt. When standing, she'd tip her head to the side, hold one hand on her hip, and shift her weight to one leg so she could elevate the other with her toes and slightly twist her knee outwards. She was a dancer. If she wasn't a child, any passing male would have thought she was being a flirt.

One Friday after school, she came over to my house to play, but she wasn't allowed to stay for dinner this time because my parents had a gig at The Tote in Collingwood that night, and I had to pack an overnight bag to stay with Tony for the weekend. So we holed up in my room and played with my stuff for an hour, which now consisted of many more porcelain ornaments and snow domes all over my bookshelf. Where my obsession for granny-flat decoration came from, or how I came into possession of it, I have no idea. Perhaps it was an attempt to be the opposite of my mother.

"Oh, I *want* this," Linda said, picking up an ornament of a ballet dancer covered in pale pink glitter.

I smiled, nodded, sat on the floor, and pulled out the drawer of Barbie dolls from under my bed. I still had the same ones and they looked pretty tattered now—especially the one with the chopped off hair.

"Oh, I don't want to play with those." Linda screwed up her nose. She took the porcelain ballet dancer in both hands and held it to her chest.

"Okay." I shrugged and pushed the drawer back under the bed. "What do you want to do?"

Linda glanced out my window, but didn't move her body an inch. "Can I have this?"

I laughed. I thought she was joking.

"Give it to me?" Linda's girly persuasive tone didn't impress me.

I frowned. "But I don't want to give it to you."

"But I want it," she said. "I'm taking it home."

"No, you're not! It's mine," I snapped.

Mum swung open my bedroom door. She had started putting makeup on, but she'd only applied foundation and drawn her eyebrows on. Her hair was really short and dark now, too. Her appearance was no longer cool to me—it was weird. My cheeks blushed.

"What's going on?" Mum said.

go

Linda threw the ballet dancer on my bed and stormed out of my room. I sat on the edge of my bed and crossed my arms.

"I've told you before, Juice, you need to stop being so bossy," Mum said.

"I wasn't bossy—" I held out the ballet dancer in my two palms. "She wanted to take this home."

"You need to learn to share."

"But it's mine!"

Mum frowned. "Linda's sitting out on the porch all by herself."

I shrugged and looked away.

"Fine." Mum sighed and left, leaving the door wide open. I got up and slammed it shut.

Why should I have to give my things away?

You shouldn't!

And I'm not bossy!

No, you're not. Mum is being mean.

Linda sat on the porch until her mum came to pick her up, but I bolted outside to apologize before she drove off, afraid that I would lose my only 'true friend.' I didn't know what I was apologizing for. It didn't feel like my fault.

But it triggered a wave of guilt.

Guilt for not giving something I was entitled to keep.

Guilt for not being selfless enough.

Guilt for being ... me.

What was it about me, when I was a child, that made other kids bully me?

Was it the blond hair that wasn't really blond and wasn't really straight and wasn't really curly? Was it the freckles that would darken and merge into small constellations and resemble patches of dirt on my skin in summer?

Was it that I feared to speak in class and often answered things incorrectly? Was it the coloured baubles on my jumper, or my chapped red lips that I'd lick and lick and lick until they cracked like the desert? Was it my voice? The way I'd extend my vowels as if they took the wrong direction in my mouth?

Was it my tears? The way they'd surface when I thought the world had it in for me? Was it the way I pulled at my sleeves and collar because I hated the feeling of wool on my skin? Was it that I'd often limp because I had flat feet?

Was it that I'd never want to share the bits of my lunch that came in shiny packets because they were rare treats for me? Was it that I'd wander aimlessly around the playground in search of someone to play with? Was it that when I found someone to play with, they'd run off on me when I looked away?

Was it that I soon gave up trying to make friends and would spend recess and lunch in the corner of the playground dragging myself along horizontal tree trunks, or jumping in and out of big black tyres, singing to myself?

Was it that I always asked to go to the toilet when I didn't have to, so that I could get away from all the staring and giggling and whispering? Was it that I'd stay in the toilet until the teacher sent someone to find me and bring me back to class?

Was it me at all?

Or was it you?

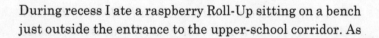

During recess I ate a raspberry Roll-Up sitting on a bench just outside the entrance to the upper-school corridor. As

go

much as I liked being alone when I chose to be, I didn't when it was forced on me. It made me feel unwanted. It didn't make sense. I wasn't able to make the connection that it was my own self-esteem issues that made me feel like this, and purposely retreat.

Mum used to tell me I could have had more friends if I hadn't been so bossy. But I didn't think I was bossy at all. I thought I was misunderstood. In my eyes, back then, I was just trying to express my point of view, not tell people what to do. The constant frustration over people always thinking and feeling the opposite of what I thought and felt, eventually caused me to shut up. Shutting up and agreeing was easier than talking and being deemed bossy.

It was an out-of-uniform day on a Friday, and my on-again-off-again 'best friend,' Linda, was playing with a bunch of other girls. I assumed she was punishing me for the unfortunate event at my house the week before.

"Fruit loop!" A freckled ginger-haired boy called out to me from two metres away as if I was emitting a deadly airborne contagion. I didn't make the connection between my multi-coloured dress and the name-calling. I just figured he was calling me crazy. My throat tensed up, and I swallowed the need to cry. It was getting easier to tame my tears in public now. All I had to do was hold up my head and close my eyes until the tension in my throat and the tickly feeling in my nose ebbed. I'm sure this gave me an 'ice queen' look, which, as the years went on, turned into ice queen behaviour.

I saw Linda and the other girls huddled in a circle about twenty metres away from me. I knew they were gossiping about me because Linda kept lifting her head and looking in my direction. Thirty seconds later, they strutted over. I swung my legs back and forth under the bench.

"You wanna come play?" Linda said. One of the other girls giggled.

I shrugged and nodded. Relieved to be asked.

We ran amongst bushes and trees—all the way to the top end of the school where hardly anyone played because it took too long to return to the assembly line when the bell rang.

"You're it!" someone said. So I faced the beige brick wall and counted to twenty.

I suspected foul play and turned around before I had finished, everyone had disappeared. They weren't hiding. They'd tricked me.

The bell rang for class and, of course, I was too far from the entrance to make it in time. Instead of rushing to the assembly line, I crept past the principal's office and snuck into line as everyone was being ushered in to the classroom like sheep.

When I saw Linda, she looked at her feet.

At home time, she called her mum to ask if I could come over for dinner.

I went. I was grateful that I had a 'true' friend.

That night after dinner, Linda's mum, Bernie, decided to take us to Timezone, a gaming hall in the centre of town, and suggested I stay the night. Bernie had tried to contact my parents at home, to ask if it was okay, but there was no answer. I thought they might have been on their way to pick me up, but because I didn't want to go home, I led Bernie to believe they would be fine with me going, and we could call them when we got back. Bernie agreed without hesitation.

But I hesitated. I knew Mum would worry if I wasn't at Linda's when she came to pick me up. But I was so eager to go out with them and have a good time, that I ignored my instincts.

go

When we got back to Linda's late at night, it was around 10 p.m. It was way past my bedtime. I didn't have school the next day, so what would the harm be?

As we walked in, Bernie told us to get ready for bed and that she'd make us a hot Milo. She pressed the button on her answering machine. There were around eight messages—from my mother.

1: Hi Bernie, it's Erika here. Just wondering when would be a good time to pick Jessica up. Give me a call.

2: Hi Bernie. It's been an hour. I thought Jessica was going straight to your house after school. Please call me and let me know when you're back.

3: We just drove by to pick up Jessica and no-one was home. Where are you?"

4: It's 9 p.m. and I still haven't heard back. If you don't call me back soon, I'll call the police.

5: Fuck. *Beep, beep, beep ...*

6: [tears] *beep, beep, beep ...*

7: *beep, beep, beep ...*

8: *beep, beep, beep ...*

Of course Bernie called home straight away and calmed her down. But when my parents picked me up the next morning, there was more to come.

"Where were you last night?" Mum snapped, as I got into the Beetle. Demetri remained silent—his usual self.

"I already said." I crossed my arms and huffed. "Time-zone!"

"I don't believe you." Mum took a deep breath as if trying to tame her rage. "I won't get angry. I just want the truth."

"But it *is* the truth."

"Jessica."

"What am I supposed to do? Lie to you so you believe me?"

"Show me some proof then."
"What do you mean?"
"Prove to me that you were at Timezone."
"How?"
"That's not my problem."
"But Bernie told you."
"I don't believe her either."

I groaned, and slumped into the seat. I numbed myself by counting the plane trees as they flitted by my window, listening to the swoosh of the cars passing us in the opposite direction. When we got home, she grounded me for a month: no TV and no Linda's after school.

A couple of weeks later, Mum asked me to put all my dirty clothes in the washing basket.

"Make sure there aren't any tissues in your pockets!" she called from the piano room[5] where I'd recently started official lessons.

I turned the pockets inside out on the blue jeans I wore at Timezone that night, and my heart raced with excitement.

Why didn't I look in my pockets for proof?

Because you're an idiot.

I ran into the backyard where Mum was hanging the first round of washing on the iron rotary clothes line. "I have proof! I *told* you! I was telling the truth!"

I held out a couple of paper tokens which you slot into the machines to activate the games. I hadn't used them all and forgot. Mum glanced at the tokens in my hand from the corner of her eye. She secured two wooden pegs with rusted springs under the sleeves of a t-shirt.

"Okay," she said, without a flinch. "You're not grounded anymore."

---

5 The glass extension that led to the toilet had now become 'the piano room.' The laundry and toilet were right next to it.

go

"Yes!" I fist-pumped the air and ran back inside. Proving her wrong and redeeming myself satisfied me to no end, but when I got back to my room, my stomach clenched with a horrible feeling of emptiness.

She grounded you when you were telling the truth. That's not fair.

But it's fixed now.

She didn't even say sorry.

Yes, but ...

How do you know if she's going to believe anything you say?

I don't know. But now I'm not grounded.

Is there any point in speaking when you aren't going to be heard?

I switched on the radio, which I'd permanently tuned to an AM radio station that played Motown Soul from the 1960s (I was obsessed with it), and sat cross-legged on my bed. I grabbed a stuffed puppy and hugged him to my chest, kissed him on the head, said "I love you," and pretended he was real.

As I grew older, I would continue to remain silent in times of conflict. And I often wonder whether the Timezone event had a role to play in the following chain of thoughts: Did I think that no-one would believe me no matter what I said? And is that why, whenever I feel depressed, I say I am fine if someone asks? And is that the reason why I, to this day, feel there is no-one on this planet I can rely on but myself? And is that the reason why I'd prefer to carry out a task myself rather than delegate it? And is that the reason I have become such a workaholic, leaving barely a second to comprehend how my career has evolved?

It does seem a bit overblown to hang all these consequential behaviours and personal theories on one small misunderstanding. I have to admit that when I hear stories about therapists digging deeply into their patients' pasts to make sense of their present, I take the results with a grain of salt. But I do know that whenever someone disbelieves what I say, I immediately think of the Timezone incident. No-one was at fault. Choices were made, words were uttered. Words and choices will always affect people in larger-than-life, inconceivable ways.

But maybe ... you know ... what if?

What if every little thing is a link in the chain?

In 1992 I was eleven, and my parents took me on a trip around Europe before heading to Ithaca, the Greek island my parents saved like scavengers to visit every few years. This would be our third visit.

We stood on a train platform in Genoa. Cloaked in toilet paper-thin plastic that the kiosks called raincoats—we looked like multicoloured sandwich bags—and watched rain gush from the gutters of the narrow shelter above us.

My stomach ached for food. It had been raining—flooding—all night, and all the shops were shut. There wasn't even anywhere to buy take-away pizza. In *Italy*. In the hostel the night before, we'd rationed one bread roll, a couple of pieces of cheese, and a tomato, between the three of us—it was the only food we had left.

My parents let me eat most of it. If not, all. Of course, *she* blamed them for letting me starve, bombarding my head with negative thoughts while I lay huddled up in the too-skinny-for-even-a-child lumpy bed. Facing a cracked crumbling wall, I opened my eyes as soon as Mum switched the light off.

go

I envisioned rain.

I imagined Mum putting her back out again.

I dreamt of her being stuck in Italy forever.

Step 1: Jump on the train, bolt down the aisle as fast as possible to find an empty cabin that we haven't booked or paid for.

Step 2: Store our bags in the railings above the seats as quickly as possible; Mum to sit upright in a window seat and stare out the window pretending not to notice any other passengers peering in; Demetri and I to sprawl our bodies over the seats so that there is no room for anyone else to sit; pretend to be asleep.

Step 3: When/If other passengers complain at our taking up all the space, Mum to shrug and apologize for our behaviour, but insist she doesn't wake us up. Under no circumstances do we open our eyes when this is happening. Demetri to snore for added effect.

Step 4: Once all passengers have boarded, and the train has been moving for a few minutes, we can 'wake up' and enjoy the trip with a whole cabin to ourselves.

Step 5: If the conductor tries to kick us out, then Mum is to cry and complain about her back problem to gain sympathy until the conductor gives in and lets us stay.

At the time, I felt it was 'mean' to not let people sit down with us. I didn't understand the need. I thought it was selfish on my mother's part. But of course, looking back on this as an adult, I don't blame her for behaving in such a way at all.

She had back pain twenty-four hours a day, and she couldn't fathom being around strangers should something go wrong. And despite her pain, and constant fear of getting a back spasm so far away from home, or running out of pills to ease her discomfort, she still insisted on travelling.

"Travel is the best education you'll ever get," she'd say.

The teachers at my school agreed and graciously prepared a homework schedule so I wouldn't fall behind.

Mum always wanted to do right by me.

That's the first thing I'll always remember about my mother. She'd bend over backwards for me to get the most out of life.

Even when it hurt.

Though there seemed to be little relief from my feelings of inadequacy in my everyday life, I still had an occasional out: the Greek island of Ithaca.

In my pre-teens, arriving to the island was like stepping foot into an enchanted pop-up fairytale book. At dawn and sunset, this Neverland of lush luminescent green mountains floating on a deep blue sea, transformed into sherbet orange skies and sharp-toothed cliffs mirrored in purple pools of water giving the impression that I could walk on the clouds—a much needed change from bullies, babysitters, recording studios, and witnessing a gradual change in Mum's behaviour that I may or may not have been conscious of, but was certainly affected by.

In the mornings, the rooster's call would wake up the locals at the first sign of sunrise. Cicadas would sing in the olive groves, and dogs would bark as the bread truck—a beat-up red Ute—would deliver fresh hot loaves to residences by slipping the required amount of bread into cloth bags hanging from wire fencing. When glittering sunlight would make patterns on my bedroom wall, Mum would make me Vegemite toast. I'd eat it on the verandah with Maria, the next door neighbour's daughter who was one year younger than me, propped up on a whitewashed ledge covered in baby blue and yellow plastic buckets, where Zacharati, Demetri's mother, would hand-wash laundry.

At midday, heat would rise in waves from the unevenly tarred road like kindred spirits before Mum and Demetri would take me to the sea—a flat, motionless bath which glowed with an infinite turquoise glint—to learn how to swim with bright orange floaties on my arms. Nikos, Demetri's father, would tend to his veggie garden, and as soon as I'd get back from the beach, Maria and I would probe the olive trees for camouflaged cicadas. As is still the case today, most folks would have a siesta between two and five in the afternoon, so there would never be much to do except wander the streets and explore.

By about 6 p.m. the sun would still be high, and the waterfront cafés would fill with shouting teenagers drinking Nescafé Frappe. I'd listen to the bells of the goats who followed their shepherds down the windy roads, butting each other's heads as they tried to escape oncoming cars and mopeds. I would ask Nikos to play cards with me on the wobbly kitchen table covered in a chequered laminate that matched the puckering brown-orange linoleum. He would show me his clever shuffling tricks with his sun-spotted hands, and I would smile and nod at his mumbling despite hardly ever understanding what he said. Zacharati would fix herself a plate of bread, feta cheese, tomato, olive oil, and oregano. She'd eat with her fingers and oil would drip down her chin and wrists.

"*Ella tho* Jessica, *ella na fas* some bread tzeez 'n' domata, is gewd for yew, ya knah!" Zacharati would summon in her high-pitched half Greek–half Australian accent due to living in Melbourne for twenty years in her prime.

She'd fumble around the kitchen with a ripped straw hat, that was maybe as old as I was at the time, greasy eighties-style sunglasses (even at night), a faded floral dress, and an overused apron.

I'll never forget the day Demetri returned from spearfishing and had brought home a massive live sea creature as big as his head, thinking it was just an empty shell. We all gathered on the verandah to take a closer look at the twenty-centimetre thick monster. With its bright red-purple veins and slippery transparent membrane, it emerged from its shell like a slimy skinless muscular arm. Zacharati suspected it was a local delicacy and promptly prepared it for the grill.

She put it in the washing machine. To tenderize it.

The whole house stank of dead fish for weeks. Thank God the washing machine was never used for its intended purpose. Most of the time it just sat, unplugged, by the toilet as an 'asset.'

We didn't end up eating the sea creature.

A local told us just in time that it was poisonous!

Mum and Demetri, now being the leaders of a new trio called Hard Candy which rocked the Melbourne indie music scene between 1992 and 1997, still managed to write music while on the island. But because they didn't have the luxury of slipping into the music room to record their ideas, they were restricted to the verandah and a cassette recorder. When writing a song, they'd play the same chords over and over, trying to perfect the chorus. And they didn't hide behind doors and leave me alone. I loved that. Everything was done out in the open and it made me feel a part of it. I'd hold onto every single good experience like a pauper to a dollar bill.

go

I had no trouble holding onto good experiences in Ithaca, until one day during our 1992 trip, when I was eleven years old, and Maria gave me her brother's bicycle so we could go cycling together.

Neither bicycles had brakes.

Of course, I thought that was okay because Maria showed me how to stop the bicycle by pushing my foot down on the spinning front wheel.

Easy peasy.

We started by riding uphill, along the old semi-paved road between the small villages of Lahos and Platreitheas, so I could practice. After resisting the urge to pick wild blackberries, we made it to the end where it branched out onto the main road. It being a small island, just 120 square kilometres, 'main road' meant 'wider road.'

We decided to head back to where we started, via the main road, because the majority of this route was downhill, and we could roll and enjoy the ride. I was exhausted after having cycled uphill for the last half an hour and my heart was pumping in my ears. I was a bit scared of 'rolling' without brakes, but there was no way I was going to show Maria my fear. She was the first friend I'd had that didn't judge me, and I wasn't going to give her a reason to. I was *not* going to be the city girl and chicken out.

Be tough.

You can do it.

She and her brother did it every day, so I could too.

I did ask her to stay close, though, without it sounding too desperate. Instead of admitting I was afraid to do it alone, I made it sound like it was no *fun* doing it alone.

She did stay close, right up until we were three large

bends away from home. Maria glided down the windy road with ease and at great speed until I could no longer see her. She disappeared, and I panicked.

I thrust my foot between the front wheel and the rod connecting the handle bars to the frame of the bicycle. As I was going pretty fast, it hurt, a lot. My heart beat even faster now as the resistance of the wind against my face strengthened. My instinct was to yank my foot out, otherwise my toes were going to be squashed and fractured.

Right at that moment, I approached a very sharp bend, and as I had picked up a lot of speed by now, my foot was no longer helping me slow down. The fear triggered a complete loss of mental and physical control. There was no way I was going to make the turn. I freaked out and launched myself off the bicycle as I took the turn too wide and knew I wouldn't make it.

The thoughts I remember flashing through my mind, before the left side of my body skidded along the gravel, narrowly missing a barbed wire fence, were:

I want my Mum.
Mum is going to kill me.
Maria left.
Everybody always runs off.

I opened my eyes. The world had shifted sideways. My head grew so heavy it felt is if it was being forced into the Earth. A neighbour screamed in terror and ran to me from across the road. My mouth and throat grew dry, and thirst crept up on me like a hot flush. I tried to speak, but no words came out.

Next thing I knew I was sitting in the backseat of a stranger's car, with a towel wrapped around my head, pulling into my grandparents' driveway.

go

Maria was waiting. She burst into tears and called for my mother. Blood dripped onto my knees as I bent forward to lean my head on the window.

"Jessicaaaaaaa!" Mum called out as though she thought I was dead.

The stranger drove us to the hospital. Mum sat by my side telling me, constantly, to keep my eyes open.

I passed out.

Next, I'm crying out in excruciating pain from a stupid doctor applying oxygen spray on my open wounds which spanned the entire left side of body.

I don't remember getting twelve stitches in my head, but I still have a raised scar that feels like there is gravel trapped under the skin of my scalp. Though I spent the next couple weeks, swollen and yellow, from head to toe, wrapped in a sheet to protect my open wounds from insects—in photos I look like an Arabian ghost with jaundice—I don't remember struggling too much. I may have actually enjoyed being injured.

I got attention. I felt cared for.

But most importantly, I felt loved.

Why do you always remind me of the bad things? I was looking at my old photo albums the other day, and there are photos of us smiling. It seems we were a happy kid. Were they honest smiles, though? Or did we smile because that's what one does *when someone has a camera in their face?*

Do photographs ever represent the genuine nature of the memories they capture? Why do we always pose? Why do we always want to look 'good' for the camera? All we are doing is lying to our future selves. Tricking ourselves into believing we were happy.

Mum follows me around with a camera in Athens when she comes to visit me and Serafeim.[6] Always in search of the perfect natural shot, she captures me in such demoralizing positions. Like with my legs spread apart on the floor, shot from my feet up so my legs look like melting tree stumps with a bad case of cellulite. But she also captures me in some flattering ones. I treasure the shots where she's captured my smile when I didn't know anyone was watching.

That is the smile I constantly crave. The smile that lights up my face and heart for no reason other than the fact I'm alive and kicking and not worried and not depressed and not thinking about the future or the past or the now. The smile that does not clutch onto expectation like a baby to a mother's breast. The smile that makes me feel like I am smiling inside as well as out, with no inhibitions, boundaries, or judgements clouding my perspective.

The smile that is absent from you *when you smile for the camera.*

In my first year at Macleod High School (later renamed Macleod College) in 1993, I turned twelve on February 26—an age hardly equipped for the transition into Year 7.

My earliest memory of high school was being late for choir class which took place before first period. As I ran up the footpath from the train station, past the expanse of green grass that students liked to litter with cigarette butts in the morning, and empty beer cans in the afternoon, the fabric of my stiff bottle-green, grey, and white chequered uniform inched up and up and up my

---

6 Serafeim is the name I have given my de facto husband in this book. We have been together since late 2005.

go

legs. Goose bumps formed on my lower legs. My knees, calves, and shins froze in the early autumn morning chill that hung over the school's massive football field as a cloud of mist. The chug chug chug of the train leaving the station echoed up the street as a kid high on some kind of narcotics yelled, "Fuck you, you fuck head, cunt."

I ignored it. Because I was late for choir. I shouldn't have hit snooze. I ran. Up the hill along the fence, spotting boys playing footy before class on the field, girls hanging around the milk bar smoking and chewing gum, the eucalyptus trees sweetening the air enough to make me sneeze and remind me of high school forever.

I was late for choir. I should have prepared lunch the night before. I ran. Through the gate and up the path, past the shelter shed and the PE change rooms, up the stairs towards my locker, never mind my locker, straight to the gym, where I'd sing, *In the jungle, the mighty jungle, the lion sleeps tonight ...*

I was late for choir. I should have left the house a minute earlier so I wouldn't have missed the early train. I ran. Through the double doors, my footsteps echoing through the gym, the entire year level standing in precise rows, mumbling amongst themselves. The teacher turned to face me and smiled. Happy to see me? No.

The whole year level stopped. Silent.

Then laughed.

I laughed too. I supposed it was funny that I was late.

"You idiot!" A voice from the back row of students startled me. My top lip twitched. Everyone pointed and giggled.

At me.

I looked down, wondering whether I was naked and being bashed with text books like in my dreams. I was not. But I'd put my windcheater on inside out and back-to-front.

I was late for choir. I should have told Mum I was sick.

I cried inside while I sung: *hush my darling, don't fear my darling, the lion sleeps tonight.*

During my first year of high school I kept to myself—much like in primary school. I was an outcast—silent, timid, afraid-of-being-noticed type—the 'fruit loop.' For months I was followed around between classes through the school corridors by giggling 'popular' girls. One of the girls in that crowd was Linda Rollins.

I was actually supposed to attend a different high school due to the town zone I lived in, but because Linda was attending Macleod, I begged Mum to try and get me into Macleod too. Linda wasn't the greatest friend, but she was my only friend, and I was scared of going to high school without someone there for support. Mum succeeded in getting me a place. But just a few weeks into the first term, Linda had started wearing makeup and hanging out with the cool kids.

She no longer wanted anything to do with me.

One day, during the last week of Year 7, I mustered an iota of courage to confront Linda and her giggling pack of hyenas. I swivelled around and all five of them stopped abruptly, laughing and bumping into each other.

"Hi Mum," said one of the girls, and flicked her hand forward as if proposing I kiss it.

"Yeah, hi Mum," said the rest of the girls in unison doing the same hand action.

I took a deep breath and gulped down menacing tears.

"Why do you do that?" I squinted at them.

They burst into laughter.

go

When about to turn around in defeat and head to my locker to change books for my next class, Linda said, "It's because you act like one. When you speak you always hang your hand like that. You look like a mum."

Linda put her hands on her hips as if she was declaring world domination. I ground my teeth together and tears pooled in the corners of my eyes.

I walked away without saying another word.

Why do you hold your hand like that?
I don't.
Yes, you do. And it looks ridiculous.
Thanks a lot.
Stop doing it. Start acting tough. You've gotta grow some balls.
Why should I? I'm fine the way I am.
Ha! You wish. You're an idiot and a wuss. Just pretend!

I left my books in my locker. I didn't go to my last class. Instead I went to the toilets—they had become my only sanctuary—and stared at myself in the mirror—my long, thick, mousy brown hair tied up in a pony tail, frizzy bits sticking up around my hairline. My pale freckled face blotchy and red from trying to hold back tears.

I smiled at myself and struck a pose with my hands on my hips.

I didn't mean to. But *she* did.

When I got home that night, I asked Mum to cut and dye my hair. I didn't need a hairdresser as Mum always cut her own and had the skill.

"Are you *sure*?" Mum said, with a huge smile on her face. I imagine she was excited to give me a makeover. All these years I wanted it long and normal—probably a subconscious reaction to not wanting to look weird like Mum. But I was starting to realize that maybe looking weird had its benefits. Clearly I wasn't like all the other girls, otherwise, why would I constantly get teased?

I had to do something about it.

"Yep. Cut it short. Not too short, but kinda long-short."

"Pixie short? With wispy bits?"

"Yeah. And then can we put red henna in it?"

Mum smiled and nodded, sat me down in the middle of the kitchen, wrapped a towel around my shoulders and held up the scissors.

"Last chance to change your mind," Mum said.

"Nah. Do it."

The swish off the metal blades swiping across each other as she opened the scissors echoed in my ears. The crunch as they sliced through my thick ponytail marked a new beginning.

No more wimpy shit.

Right. No more wimpy shit.

It wasn't long before I got my nose pierced.

I was ready to rock Year 8.

part two
1994-1996

part two
1991-1996

go

By the beginning of Year 8, the teasing subsided a bit, and I started hanging out with a group of 'nerds.' I liked them, and we got on at school, but I still didn't fit in. I wasn't as smart as the nerds, and I wasn't as pretty as the popular girls. It made me feel even more inferior.

This meant I still kept to myself most of the time, and hated participating in team projects. But keeping my mouth shut and not being 'bossy,' also meant I avoided voicing my opinion when it mattered most. My grades in Maths, Biology, Social Sciences, and German averaged around a C, with the random D thrown in. In artsy subjects like Metalwork, Textiles, and Drama, which required quiet creative time, I'd often get As. And in English I averaged around a B because I'd always get top marks in assignments I was able to do on my own.

It didn't matter. It was better to get subpar grades in the 'important' subjects than it was to speak and risk being ridiculed. But then I connected with two girls, Tracy and Laurel, who didn't belong in any kind of peer group at all—just like me. They were sisters with different surnames, one a year older, but both in the same year level as me, as the elder one had been kept down for poor grades. Laurel was the younger one. She had mousy-brown shoulder-length hair, blue eyes, and buck teeth. Tracy had darker hair, almost black, with deep brown eyes, and was a little chubbier. Somehow, when Tracy sniffed, her nostrils would close and vibrate against each other. I'm sure she did it on purpose to make everyone squirm.

They caught my full attention one day in English class.

"This is fucked!" Laurel said, and slammed her text book closed. "I don't understand shit about this fuckin' book!" Everyone in the class laughed, except Tracy, who smirked silently, one side of her mouth turning upwards with pride.

"Laurel, gather your things and go to the principal's office, please. I will not tolerate that kind of language in my classroom," Mrs Flannery said, with utter calm, looking above her glasses at a clipboard she had hooked in one arm. Laurel burst into laughter. I'm sure her voice carried all the way to the school's football field which was at least a kilometre away.

When she got up to leave, one of the fat Italian boys threw a pen at her and it hit her in the head.

"Hey!" Mrs Flannery barked. "That's enough. Apologize."

Laurel swivelled round and put a hand on her hip. She said, "Don't worry, Miss. I can handle this." She pursed her lips and thrust her middle finger up with such gusto you could practically hear it pierce the air.

Mrs Flannery held her arm out and pointed to the door. "Out!" she shouted.

"With fuckin' pleasure," Laurel said.

In the next class, I sat with Tracy and Laurel at the back of the room. They glanced at me. I smiled. They smiled back.

"Fuck," Laurel said under her breath, as she rummaged through her pencil case. "I forgot my fuckin' rubber."

Tracy said, "Use mine."

"There's nothin' left to fuckin' hold of *yours*."

I took one of mine out of my pencil case and handed it to her.

"Keep it," I said. "I've got two."

From that moment forward, we hung out together. And every time I hung out with them, I'd feel like I was doing something wrong—and that gave me a thrill. I'd

go

go to their house after school, chill out in the bungalow in their backyard—which was their bedroom—listened to Ace of Base, because even though I hate to admit it, I liked pop music before turning into a grunge head. (A great pop tune still gets me dancing.) They'd tell me their secrets. Like how Laurel's last stepfather molested her, and that's why they had a new one.

I felt empowered to know these things because it meant they trusted me.

And I trusted them.

I'd even enjoy eating dinner with their family. We ate things like Uncle Bill's sweet and sour sauces with rice—not that healthy stuff my parents liked to cook from scratch, like vegetable pie and zucchini slice, over and over and over, foods that I still can't eat to this day without feeling an overwhelming sense of boredom and helplessness. At Tracy and Laurel's, it always seemed like I was eating junk food, and that was such a treat.

I grew to love these sisters like sisters of my own, though I think, in their eyes, I was the conservative little girl they'd challenged themselves to convert into a rebel. Even if on a subconscious level. It wasn't my time yet, but it didn't mean I didn't enjoy watching them in action. Though, their mother—from whom they definitely learnt how to swear—once had a go at me for wearing Blundstone boots with my summer school uniform. My excuse? It was the trend. And I knew that because Mum's female friends wore them with skirts too. I was definitely on my way to becoming 'cooler.'

I finally had friends. True friends that didn't give a shit about what other people thought of them. They were at thirteen and fourteen what many wish they could be at thirty. Sure of themselves, taking 'no shit from nobody,' doing what they wanted within their means, and just being themselves without any shame or need to behave the way society thought they should.

Because of Tracy and Laurel, I learnt that no-one has control over anything, so just do what you feel is right in the moment. Don't stop to think. Don't second guess yourself. Just do it.[7]

The next time someone bothered me in the school corridor, I held my own.

A muscly blonde guy with a face full of acne bumped into me on purpose as I was putting books in my locker. They tumbled out of my arms and onto the floor.

He laughed and said, "Gull-i-ball." The word *gullible* lengthened and pronounced like he'd hit slo-mo on the remote. A habit picked up by the jocks after they'd play pranks on people. Clearly this kid hadn't grasped the true meaning of the word.

I thought back to the time I was a little kid and Mum told off that bully at the bus stop. I turned around and squinted at the guy, now buckled over from laughing, because obviously, this was the funniest moment in his world.

I said, "Go fuck yourself." I didn't look him in the eye.

"Oooh, I'm so scared." He wagged his head side to side with exaggeration.

"You should be," I said, swivelling around to meet his gaze. "Because if you touch me again, I'll slice your penis off in the PE change rooms."

I'm not sure how successful that was in stopping the bullying, but it certainly felt good. It was one of the most triumphant feelings I'd ever experienced up to that point. I slowly grew more confident, more in control of my life, and found the strength to let the verbal abuse slide off

---

[7] Nike has not paid me to say that.

my back. And for a while I stopped caring what anyone thought of me.

Unfortunately, that didn't last long.

It happened on September 17, 1994, five months after Kurt Cobain shot himself.

I lurked around the kitchen table at Tony's place—doing who knows what—eating snacks?—when the phone rang. Margaret answered in her usual jolly tone, but then her voice dropped to a whisper.

"Oh hi Demetri! ... oh ... uh huh ..." She passed the phone to Tony, glanced at me and then wiped her hands on her apron, probably out of nervousness. She hid her feelings well. I had no idea anything was going on.

"Hello?" Tony pushed his glasses up his nose. "Aw ... yeah. Okay. Yup, sure." Tony hung up, cleared his throat, and adjusted his glasses once more.

"Gotta take you home, Possum." He grabbed a set of keys off the hook on the wall by the phone.

"Why?" I didn't want to go home. I wanted to spend the weekend messing about with Allison and Geoffrey.

"Come on. Your mum'll tell ya at home."

I collected my things and got in the car. I was excited. I thought they had a surprise for me. Like they were going to send me on the school trip to Bali they'd recently said they couldn't afford. Or maybe we were going to Greece again and they wanted me to come and pack. All sorts of scenarios sifted through my head.

I listed all these things out loud for Tony during the drive. He chuckled. But it wasn't a happy one. It was a chuckle that embodied nervous pity.

Right then I knew it wasn't good news.

Maybe something happened to Mum.

Relax, I'm sure everything is fine.

But what about her back? Maybe it's worse this time. Maybe she's paralysed!

You're being stupid. Calm down.

But ...

Chill out, will you?

I stared out the window in silence for the rest of the drive home. When we arrived, he walked me to the front door, but didn't come in. Demetri thanked him. I stepped inside. Mum was sitting in a kitchen chair—because it was the only type of seat that supported her back properly—in the middle of the living room. She sobbed, wiping tears away with overused tissues that had disintegrated all over her face. She held out her hand and gestured for me to come close, her nose shining red in the dimmed orange lamp light, her fringe sweaty and stuck to her forehead.

I can't remember the exact words she used to tell me that Laurel had died from a brain haemorrhage. I burst into tears before Mum had a chance to finish the sentence, and fell into her embrace. She cradled me in her arms for I don't know how long. The pain in my chest was like someone had reached inside me, replaced my blood with water, my heart with ash, and my soul with smoke.

I didn't understand. How does a person's brain just start to bleed?

Why weren't there any signs?

She was her usual crazy self at school.

I had lost a person I could confide in—and though I couldn't put it into words at the time—I was sure I'd lose Tracy, as well, to grief. I did. Our relationship was never the same, and she dropped out of school a year later.

go

I stayed in bed the whole weekend bawling my eyes out. I put Laurel's school photo in a frame and treated it like a shrine. I spoke to her. I told her that I was *so* sorry. I didn't know what I was sorry for. I ached for her, I think, more than myself. She lost her life so unexpectedly. *She* lost. Not me. *She* lost everything. It hurt so deep inside me that she wouldn't become an adult, that we wouldn't have the chance to rebel against the world together.

Mum let me be for a couple of days, but then forced me to get out of bed. I didn't want to. The world had become an utterly useless and hopeless place within seconds, even more so than I already believed. She talked about the funeral, how there would be an open casket, and that I shouldn't be afraid.

"She'll just look like she's sleeping," she said.

Then came the clincher.

Mum and Demetri had to go on tour in Sydney for their latest album, *Lick*[8], and they wouldn't be able to come with me. I stayed with Tony and Margaret. Tony took me to the funeral. I tried to not let it bother me at the time, but it's something that has stayed with me my whole life.

At the funeral, I approached the open casket with Tony by my side. When Laurel's face came into view, cushioned by deep red velvet padding, a very quiet sound escaped Tony's mouth as if he'd been punched in the stomach, but was trying to hide his reaction. From the corner of my eye, I saw him reach out to hug me around my shoulders. But before he made contact, I said, "She looks dead."

He retracted his hand and stifled a laugh. More out of embarrassment, I assume, than anything else. I don't know if he understood why I said that. I didn't bother to explain.

---

[8] You can watch Hard Candy perform 'Push You,' a track off the *Lick* album, live at The Evelyn Hotel here: *bit.ly/HardCandyAU1*

I searched her face for evidence of a brain bleed. I needed to understand the physics of her death. I wanted to see inside her head—each and every tiny detail that resulted in this day. Sure enough, some evidence was there. Faintly showing through layers and layers of makeup that made her look like a wax sculpture, were patches of purple bruising. They weren't wholly visible, but there was just enough to make me hold my breath. I thought about the pain she must have suffered the morning she died on the couch in her living room. She'd complained of a bad headache and her mother gave her an aspirin and told her to lie down.

An aspirin. I didn't know this at the time, but it would have been the aspirin that caused the clot to burst. I can only imagine what her mother would have gone through after discovering this.

I didn't intend to, but because everyone was staring and waiting for me to move on so others could say goodbye, I kissed Laurel on her forehead.

Her skin felt like cold concrete on my lips.

"I wanna go home," I said to Tony, my stomach going queasy. He nodded in silence. I'm sure he was just as clueless about what to do in this situation.

I wanted my mum.

But she wasn't there.

And soon she would be absent a lot more.

October, 1994, my speech at Laurel's Memorial at Macleod High School

```
Laurel you were such a fantastic girl.
```

go

And for the years I've known you, you've always loved to laugh.

You cracked jokes.

You'd chase boys.

You'd run around the school yard going totally out of this world.

And there's one thing for sure, you'd always understand people. You listened.

You always knew what to say. You cared.

And Laurel, you will always be in my heart, your large and wonderful smile will always be in my memories.

I love you Laurel, and goodbye.

A couple of months after Laurel's death, I found music waiting by our front door.

Mum had decided to list her twelve-string acoustic guitar for sale in the *Trading Post*. Demetri had many guitars, so it seems odd to me now why she wanted to get rid of her oldest and most-cherished instrument. They probably needed their electric guitars to record albums, and so the twelve-string had less practical use.

I assume they decided to sell it because they'd found another parking fine trapped under a windscreen wiper. As far as I can remember, this happened many times, especially when they played a gig and needed to park in convenient (illegal) spaces to transport their music equipment to gig venues without breaking their backs.

Well. I saw the twelve-string sitting by the front door. My parents were expecting someone to come and take a look. What actually happened when I saw the twelve-string by the door is lost somewhere in my personal mythology. But the way I remember it is this:

I opened the case and touched the glossy wooden body, running my fingers over the taut strings, admiring the creamy mother of pearl markers on the frets—though at the time I thought they functioned as mere decoration. This treasure, lying so snug inside the velvety red lining of its battered and faded black case, was something I *needed* to have. I couldn't understand how Mum could part with it. Surely something else could have been sold—something a little less special?

Mum's extended vocal belted from the music room. I knew she was recording, but I couldn't stop myself from interrupting her.

I opened the door and poked my head inside. Mum stopped mid-note and switched off the four-track mixer. I thought she might be annoyed with me, but she just stared, waiting for me to speak.

"Can I have the guitar?" I said.

Mum dropped her hands to her sides, paused a moment, then smiled. "If you learn to play it," she said, "then you can have it."

So I taught myself how to play.

For weeks I messed about on one string creating simple melodies. I'd play these melodies over and over until the muscle memory was so ingrained I didn't even have to know what notes I plucked. I still don't know the notes I play on guitar. I learnt by ear. Never have I looked at a sheet of music or tablature to learn a song, or recorded the notes of a song in written form, in all my life. If I write a song, I memorize it, until I can record it in audio.

As I wrote my first song, déjà vu warmed my bones. I was nine years old again, painting flowers on the dark blue Beetle in our backyard. I'd found another place to run to, another place to hide. A process of internalizing the world around me. I no longer had to take any real responsibility for my feelings, because my feelings were now art.

Music became the only way I knew how to express myself. A way to gather the darkness that simmered inside me. And by regurgitating that darkness into a neat little three-minute package that could potentially be *enjoyed*, I was hidden in plain sight.

And no-one would ever understand a thing.

Because 'it's just a song.'

The bottom E took the lead in the first two songs I ever wrote. The bottom E was technically two strings tuned to the same note, but an octave apart. The riffs I wrote were more bass lines and were rhythmic enough to sing a typical verse-chorus-verse-chorus song structure over them.

What follow are lyrics from the first page of my lyric book—a hardcover notebook with a black and white picture of a little boy giving a little girl a red rose (the rose being the only thing in colour). They are both reaching in to kiss each other, so close their lips are almost touching, but not. Scribbled on the cover, in blue biro, is the shape of a bird, which could also be interpreted as a bow and arrow, right above the boy's groin. There is also a spear-like scribble sticking into his knee.

Going Crazy (dated 1994, spelling mistakes included)

```
I feel like I'm going crazy
I'm always walking in the rain
Almost everything is boring
Just like playing lots of games
```

```
Maybe I'm just getting older
Maybe I'm feeling too ashamed
Of what I don't know
Caring for people doesn't do much good
It just makes me know more and more
I'm much too lonely

Chorus
All the things I do
I work to hard for
There's no way that I'm going to live x 2


I live alone
That's obviously why I'm lonely
I don't have many friends
Don't ask me why because I don't know
The only friends I have are dead
Why did they have to leave me
I didn't do anything wrong
One was killed and one died natruly

Chorus x2
V1
Chorus

Why did they, why did they, why did they all
have to leave me x 4
```

One night in early 1995, when I had turned fourteen, I had two high school acquaintances visit. Tim and Nelly were a part of the grungy crowd. I had started hanging out with them during recess and lunch, not 'officially,' but sort of as a guest, so I was eager to impress. I'd invited them over to play a couple of my songs thinking it would help me be accepted into their peer group. But a part of me knew it was a cry for acceptance on a much deeper level.

I wanted them to understand how lonely I felt without saying it out loud. I wanted them to take me under their wings, understanding this aspect of me, without acknowledging the fact directly. But what I wanted, overall, was a form of love that seemed to be missing from my life and I thought I might be able to receive it through another person's admiration.[9]

No-one other than my parents had heard the songs, so I'd also prepared myself for ridicule. But it was a gamble I was willing to take as I didn't think I could feel any more hollow than I already did. I knew I had work to do, because even though Mum said she was really impressed and encouraged me to keep writing, I think she gushed over my enthusiasm and effort rather than the songs themselves, as she would always say that practice made perfect.

You're attention seeking.

I'm just sharing something that means a lot to me.

You're attention seeking. Keep this up and you'll be popular in no time.

I'm not doing it to be popular.

Bullshit. Come on. Can you honestly say you don't want the attention?

I uh ...

I took a deep breath, and played my songs sitting cross-legged on the carpet. Remembering the pee stain in the corner, and that Tim might actually be sitting on it, my

---

[9] I'm convinced this is a DNA defect. No matter how much love I am given, I rarely feel it. It's like when a kid eats and eats and eats, and never gains weight, and is deemed to have 'hollow legs.' My legs are hollow when it comes to consuming love.

right leg shook and my voice trembled. Tim pushed his waxy blond dreadlocks out of his dark brown eyes and smiled compassionately at my nervousness. It calmed me down having noticed that he noticed.

When I finished both songs, Nelly said something simple, along the lines of, "I like them. They sound cool," and nodded in approval.

"Really?" I said. "Thanks." I looked at her orange fingers, trying to distract myself from the growing feeling of disappointment by wondering why she didn't wear gloves before dying her hair.

I eagerly anticipated Tim's response, hoping it would be something a little more gushing. Tim chuckled and covered his mouth with his hand. He often covered his mouth. He was probably self-conscious about his crooked teeth, but I thought they made him look sweet and kind.

I said, "What's funny?" with a bit of a nervous chuckle.

He said, "They both sound the same," hesitating after the word 'both.'

"Tim!" Nelly punched him in the shoulder and frowned. "Nah, they're cool," she said. "Don't listen to 'im."

I prayed that Nelly wasn't just being polite and had heard how the beat of my heart paused at every transition between verse and chorus, with every lyric written as a silent plea to be heard and understood, with every note that didn't quite make it to the finish line, but begged to claim a piece of the spotlight.

But I *didn't* get the desired praise. And their lack of enthusiasm *did* make me feel more hollow.

Tim was right. On the surface both songs sounded the same.

What was different, was me.

Loneliness had found another way to feed.

go

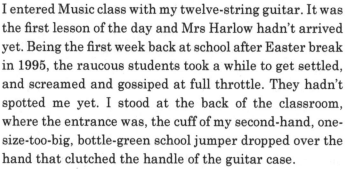

I entered Music class with my twelve-string guitar. It was the first lesson of the day and Mrs Harlow hadn't arrived yet. Being the first week back at school after Easter break in 1995, the raucous students took a while to get settled, and screamed and gossiped at full throttle. They hadn't spotted me yet. I stood at the back of the classroom, where the entrance was, the cuff of my second-hand, one-size-too-big, bottle-green school jumper dropped over the hand that clutched the handle of the guitar case.

I lowered the case to the dark blue carpeted floor and laid it flat. I flicked open the brass latches, the last one clicking as Mrs Harlow stepped foot inside. She looked at me from above and attempted a smile, but as usual, it appeared like she was trying to dislodge something from her teeth.

"Right. Hush!" Mrs Harlow clapped her hands to get everyone's attention. "Jessica has graciously agreed to play us one of her original songs today, so please close your books and put your pens away. And hush."

If it wasn't for Mrs Harlow, I imagine there would have been a few groans and snickers. Maybe even teasing remarks. But students were afraid of Mrs Harlow. She was one of those lucky teachers who was able to control her pupils like no other teacher in the school. Which was a feat at Macleod High, because many kids—the boys especially—were extremely loud and obnoxious.

I lifted my twelve-string out of its case and stood up. Mrs Harlow gestured to the front of the classroom. I chose to sit in the first row, so I could face my back to everyone. I pulled a chair out far enough to fit the guitar between me and the edge of the desk.

What are you doing?

I can't look at them.
They'll make fun of you for it.
I don't care, they can say whatever they like.

Someone in the back row giggled.

"Shoosh!" Mrs Harlow raised a finger to her lips. "Respect."

The guilty student cleared their throat and shut up.

I began to play without introducing the song ... the plectrum ticked over the bottom two strings—a heartbeat escaping from my fingertips. A few hushed snickers from the back row made my high vocals crack. My knees shook up and down. The rough plastic of the chair collided with the goose bumps on my legs, but the rhythm of my strumming remained steady.

```
she sits on a step in the city square
staring at people from everywhere
they stare back in a real bad way
like they want to kill her because she's gay
```

As the word *gay* was strung out in an extended sliding note, from high to low, someone scoffed.

Fuck them.
It's just a song.

I had chosen the one that expressed feelings of discrimination about being gay, not because I thought I was—yet—but because I thought Mrs Harlow would latch onto the fact that I'd explored an important issue and commend me for it.

I couldn't have been more wrong.

As I strummed the final note, silence followed by trickles of unenthusiastic applause and bad attempts at stifling laughter, especially from the boys.

I stood up, and walked through the centre aisle towards

the back of the room, in what seemed like slow motion. A couple of girls whispered to each other, one guy put two fingers to his lips and wriggled his tongue between them, another girl with frizzy hair and thick glasses had her hands folded in front of her and her eyes closed.

I reached my guitar case, placed the guitar inside, and secured the brass latches.

Click, click, click.

"Well done, Jessica," Mrs Harlow said. "But please make a note, everyone, that although songs sometimes repeat verses as well as choruses, it isn't done as often as Jessica has done so in hers today."

Had my parents been humouring me when they said my songs were good? The comment was like a stab in the back. According to my lyric book, I wrote nine songs between 1994 and 1995. The next date I have written on a separate page, all on its own, as *Start Again, 1996*. Did this incident pull me away from writing for a whole nine months? I can't remember. But I guess the 'Start Again' is rather telling.

Giving up wasn't an option.

In July of 1995, my parents took me out of school for three months and we headed to Ithaca again. This time with a rigorous homework schedule that chained me to my books for many hours of the day. I especially resented my mum for this, as she was the only one who'd discipline me. It didn't help that my escalating puberty blues had now begun to cause a deep rift in our relationship. Every single thing Mum said, whether related to me or not, I would challenge. Every time she'd try to show me affection, I would shrug her off. When she'd complain about being in pain, I would roll my eyes. When she ran out of Valium one day, and freaked out in the middle of the night because the only doctor we had on the island was away for a couple of days, I wished she would just die.

I lay in bed one night, staring at the ceiling, listening to her ranting and crying in the bedroom next door.

"What am I going to do? I can't be without them. I'm going to jump out of my skin. We have to go home. We have to go back to Australia. Demetri! Stop nodding and *do* something!"

"Erika, he'll be back tomorrow. Can you please calm down?"

"Calm down? Do you have any idea what this *feeeels* like? I can't cope. I can't cope. I'll kill myself. I'll kill myself, you just watch me!"

She should just do it. Life would be better without her.

Something thumped against the wall. I held my breath and buried my face into my pillow and pulled the covers over my head. I feared she'd smashed her head against the wall.

Silence.

Please be okay please be okay please be okay.
Who gives a shit if she's okay.
I do.
No, you don't.
Shut up!

Their bedroom door opened and I heard Zacharati's high pitched voice, trying to whisper. I didn't hear what she said, but the three of them rushed out. I jumped out of bed and followed, but far enough behind so they couldn't see me.

Mum, breathing frantically, ran outside, through the garden and out the back gate. Demetri bolted after her, and I ran after him. When they'd reached the front of

go

Maria's house, they paused. I hid behind the side wall and listened.

"I can't wait until morning. I'm just going to do it."

"Erika, don't."

"Can't you see me?"

"You're just scared. Tomorrow morning you'll be fine."

"I'm not, Demetri. I am *sick*." Mum spat the word *sick* as if it had tasted bitter. "I'm in *pain*. Can't you see?"

I didn't hear another word, but when I poked my head around the corner of the house, they had disappeared.

For some reason their behaviour left me feeling embarrassed and ashamed. I did everything in my power to not spend time with my mum. I didn't want to know what was going on with her. I didn't want to be thrust into a position which made me feel the push and pull of my own conflicting emotions. I hated myself for wishing she'd kill herself.

What kind of daughter thinks that?

You do.

It's you who thinks that, not me.

Listen carefully ... our voice is one.

Most days I'd lock myself in my room to do my school reading, and then hang out in Stavros Square with the local island kids. They were so sheltered and 'normal,' I relished every moment of their simple no-frills existence: wake up, eat, go to the beach, nap, eat, hang out in the square until midnight. Repeat.

I didn't want to go back to Australia. I wanted to live on Ithaca and have a million European summers in a row. But most of all, I wanted the escape from my parents—and my own head—that Ithaca provided.

Having the freedom to remove myself from my parents' lives led to two important life changes:

1) I read *A Long Way from Verona*, by Jane Gardam, a novel about a girl named Jessica Vye whose 'violent experience' colours her schooldays and her reaction to the world around her. Interestingly, Jessica Vye was told that she is 'beyond all possible doubt,' a born writer—an aspect of the story line I had completely forgotten until I looked up the book to find the name of the author. It was the first time I'd ever been hooked on a novel so much that I struggled to put it down at night. This enlightened me, because even though I loved writing songs, and the occasional poem inspired by the Greek landscape, I didn't think much of it as something to excel in. It inspired me to choose English Literature as one of my electives the following school year. That, compulsory English—which was more focussed on writing argumentative essays on current affairs—and Drama, were the only subjects I thrived in. I didn't even do well in Music because I hated reading sheet music and my disinterest in theory inhibited me. Though I had not made the decision to pursue writing as a career yet, this established a foundation for something I would explore at university.

2) I had my first kiss. I wrote a poem about it in 2012, and published it in my collection, *Fabric*:

Soap & Silk

```
Our sweaty palms blend
like moist tongues—
they swing between
two shaking pairs
of legs; goat bells
jingle through thistly leaves,
introducing the speed
of a passing moped.
```

go

He looks left
He looks right
He looks up and down
the lampless street.
I grit my teeth
when his eyes focus
on the tip
of my nose
—or is it my top lip?

He grabs my breast
adorned in green
olive silk—he leans
toward me, camel breath—
tobacco ripe.
A pack of cigs
hits the ground
when our front teeth collide.
He vacuums my tongue
into a hole, I wish
I could wash
out with soap.
Bitter flushes
the rear of my throat.

I pull away, swallow,
wince, and vow
to never kiss
a 'God'
again.

Despite this awkward first kiss, and the tension with Mum, life remained carefree on Ithaca. I could be out

at any time of day, at any place I wanted, without any curfew or inconvenient worry from my parents. The environment was one hundred per cent safe. Like a tiny little planet independent from Earth.

Not long after my first kiss, I got my hair cut really short—almost crew-cut style. I felt more alternative and mature, and believed it suited my goal to become a rock star. Yup. That was my dream. I was becoming a 'proper' person, and I was proud of myself. Proud that life was moving forward in the way it was supposed to. And even though I still felt an overwhelming sense of hopelessness in life from time to time, I managed to ignore it for a while. Perhaps that's why I didn't write songs again until 1996. Because I didn't feel the need to run and hide.

I figured there were so many possibilities, so many opportunities, and a whole future ahead of me, that if I didn't like something, I could just do something else. The melancholy that seeped into my creative projects was merely a backdrop now. It lingered. Made me cry. But I'd always get back up when it was over, and keep taking another step forward.

Unfortunately, it didn't take long for that pride to be crushed. Village boy didn't like the new haircut and told all his friends I looked like a goat.

Now, not only could I not keep friends, I couldn't keep boyfriends, either.

I spent the last month on the island praying for my hair to grow out. I wanted to go back to Australia, where short hair on a girl was considered cool and not likened to a herd animal.

Yes, I wanted to go home—the place I had wanted to run from. I realized then that I was more comfortable living amongst the complexities of eccentricity, the drama of reality, and the unknown, yet promising, status of a potential high school social life.

At least it was a place I could be anyone I wanted to be. Fake it till you make it, right?

Back in Australia, in early 1996, before my fifteenth birthday, my parents invited friends over for a Saturday night drink—Melanie, Mum's back-up vocalist, and her new boyfriend, Sean. An Aussie-Greek eccentric called Patrick, who they'd met on Ithaca the year prior during drunken escapades, also turned up. I sat in the living room with them, assuming their drinking and smoking and chemically induced laughing was normal behaviour. I had fun watching them, being around them; it made me feel cool to have cool parents. And to top it off, their friends were like aunts and uncles to me because they treated me as one of their own. (It also helped that one day when Demetri picked me up from school, a student asked if he was the drummer of Faith No More. I said, "Yeah, he came all the way from America to pick me up." This felt like a social leg up.)

I'm sure Mum thought she'd hidden the pot smoking from me by sending everyone into the backyard to smoke it, but I knew what it smelled like. I wasn't stupid. After all, my high school took its nickname, Mull-cleod High, from the slang for the tobacco mix used with marijuana.

I overheard a conversation between Mum and Patrick as I approached the kitchen to grab myself some lemon squash. The door was open an inch, and I peeked through the gap. Patrick was begging her for a Valium, wiggling his lanky limbs around like they were about to fall off. His dead-straight shoulder-length hair was hooked behind his ears, accentuating his Mediterranean nose. "*Come on, Erika,*" I heard him say, among other things, in his nasally but charming voice, in an attempt to persuade her to give him one. I don't know if she was reluctant to give him one because she was running out, or whether she thought it would do him harm. In the end she gave him one. It was to relieve his rib and back pain—which, I seem to recall, turned out to be a hairline fracture in his ribs from a drunken summer fall on Ithaca.

As the night went on, and Mum began to sway from side to side every time she stood up, she disappeared for longer than it would take to top her glass up with vodka.

"Where's Mum?" I asked Patrick.

"Uh ... she'll be back in a minute."

"But where is she?"

"You don't want to go out there," he said with a chuckle.

I made my way through the kitchen, the glass extension I had now shaken my fear of, and into the backyard.

Mum hung from her hips over one of the supporting bars of my now unused orange and lime-green swing set. Her body hung limp in the shape of the Greek letter Λ, the ends of her now shoulder-length red hair stroking her chunky vomit in the grass with each heave.

I walked over to her, rubbed her back, and tried to get her to stand up so I could help her to bed.

"Don't tell Mum," she said in the voice of a child. "I'm not allowed to drink."

I stayed out there for a few minutes, holding her hair out of her face, as she vomited. Though I wanted to care for her, I was really tired and needed to go to bed. I had homework to do the next day.

My parents' friends passed through the backyard on their way out and wished us good luck. Demetri helped

go

me get Mum to bed. We guided her in silence. Demetri was either too out of it to say anything coherent, or simply being his usual silent self. I didn't know what to say, but not out of anger or disappointment. I had disassociated myself from the situation. I made the necessary moves as if being controlled by a remote, even though I had never done this before. My ability to block out emotionally challenging experiences had switched itself on without any conscious provocation.

Demetri and I sat Mum on the edge of her bed, and I stood up, assuming this was all I was required to do.

"Don't leave me," Mum pulled on my arm. "Please stay."

I glanced at Demetri.

"I'm gonna tidy up," he said, pushing his long black curls out of his face. "Won't be long." He wobbled down the hallway in his bare feet, skinny black jeans, and shirt with a flamboyant green, white, and black pattern, and closed the kitchen door behind him.

I lay down next to Mum. Demetri brought a wet face cloth, a towel, a bucket to throw up in, and left them on the floor. The stench of fermented pizza and alcohol emphasized the foulness of the chunky splash as her vomit hit the bottom of the bucket. When it seemed she had nothing left in her stomach but bile, she held her nostrils closed and tried to breathe through them.

"I can't breathe," she said, panic creeping into her nasally voice. "What's wrong with me? I can't breathe."

"Stop holding your nose and you'll be able to breathe," I said.

She shook her head from side to side, still pinching her nose closed. "I can't breathe. Help. I can't breathe."

"Breathe through your mouth," I said. If she wasn't going to stop holding her nose closed, it seemed like a logical thing to tell her to do.

She shook her head again. "Nope. It's not natural to breathe through your mouth. I need to breathe through my nose."

"Then let go of your nose, Mum." I rested my head on Demetri's pillow. It smelt of Sunsilk conditioner and methylated spirits.

"Don't tell my mum, okay?" she said again in a sleepier tone. "I'll get punished."

"I won't." My head sank farther and farther into Demetri's pillow as I focussed on the sound of clinking dishes coming from the kitchen.

Mum released her nose and took a long deep breath through her nostrils.

"Better?" I said.

She nodded and smiled—"I still can't breathe."—and held her hand to her head. "Don't tell my mum, okay?"

"I *promise*." I rolled my eyes. "I won't tell your mum."

For a moment I thought how cool this story was going to sound when I retold it at school on Monday. I pictured myself in my mother's shoes, Tim or Nelly nursing me like I nursed her. I imagined the stories that would spread about me, how I might actually be considered cool, and maybe a rebel. Maybe if I got drunk in front of my peers, I would become a 'real' teenager, and more people would want to hang out with me.

I decided. I would get drunk at the next party I was invited to.

I sat up to check if Mum was falling asleep. Her eyes were closed and her chest rose and fell at a normal pace. Demetri returned. We exchanged glances and I slinked off the bed. We hugged each other goodnight and I tiptoed to my bedroom.

Being alone in my bed had never felt so good.

go

I don't know why she told me she couldn't breathe after she clearly could. Maybe it was code for something else. Maybe she couldn't breathe in this *world*.

Maybe the world was suffocating her, as I felt it was suffocating me.

Friday afternoon, the following week, I sat in the middle of my bedroom floor listening to the movements being made in the house.

On the right, towards the music room ...

... the clicking of guitar leads as they unwound

... the crack of a lead being plugged into an amplifier

... the *one tzew tzew* of Demetri's voice testing the volume of the microphone, the tuning of his Les Paul, the accidental feedback, Mum clearing her throat and muttering, "Is the tape in?"

Then the sound I was waiting for: the door to the music room clacking shut.

I rummaged through my school bag and pulled out the empty water bottle I'd been saving, inched open my bedroom door, tip-toed into the living room and closed the door behind me.

I twisted the cap off my water bottle and poured in an inch of Stolichnaya, an inch of Cointreau, an inch of Bombay Sapphire Gin, an inch of Ouzo, and an inch of Drambuie.

When Demetri dropped me off at the party, he told me to be good. He always said 'be good' like he didn't really know what he was asking. It was just what parents were supposed to say, right?

Be good.

What does that mean exactly?

I walked through the long corridor of Nelly's incense-infused house and into her backyard, pulled out my concoction and took a big swig. I hid the bottle back in my bag as I didn't want people asking what it was. The sting of the potent spirits didn't make me wince, instead it warmed my chest with an intense feeling of *release*.

Tim offered me a cigarette, flicking his dreadlocks to one side of his face. I glanced at the knee-wide rips in his light blue jeans, hesitating before taking the cigarette.

Tim chuckled. "You smoke?"

I didn't. It was my first one.

I shrugged. "Only at parties."

"Cool," Tim said, jolting. Nelly had pushed a stubbie into his neck with her blue-black fingers—she'd dyed her hair again. She poked him in the ribs and he took the beer.

I put the cigarette in the left corner of my lips.

"Nell, you gotta light?"

"Sure." She pulled a box of Red Head matches out of her back pocket. "Wanna beer too?"

I nodded with a half smile, trying to act cool, as I struck a match against the box and lit the cigarette as Nelly went back inside.

On the first drag I coughed and spluttered, but managed to control it and hide it enough for it to look like it wasn't the cigarette's doing. So I thought. A few kids I didn't know turned around and looked at me. One very tall girl, with a masculine build, smirked. Our glances collided momentarily before I flicked my head in the opposite direction. My stomach turned with embarrassment as I realized I was sitting on the edge of Nelly's slightly raised garden bed all on my own. I had to make up for this minor deflation in my yet-to-be-established reputation.

go

"All good?" Nelly said, approaching with a VB stubbie. I nodded. She gave me two thumbs up and walked over to Tim who was now on the other side of the yard, laughing and drinking with a bunch of blokes who were talking about some neighbour with big white tits.

I swigged my beer intermittently, staring at the tufts of trampled brown grass that grew through the cracks in the ground. Cigarette butts and pieces of broken brown glass adorned the perimeter of a harassed tree whose roots tried to break free through the concrete.

I held each drag of the cigarette in my mouth, without inhaling it. I'd tilt my head to the right and slightly upward when I exhaled. That was how the other girls were doing it.

I got tipsy pretty fast and remember thinking I could do anything—that I was invincible. No wonder my mother told me she used to drink a whole bottle of vodka before a gig.

It really did make you feel like a rock star.

Rage Against the Machine's 'Killing in the Name' blared through Nelly's back door.

I nodded my head to the strict heavy beat, the words *Fuck you I won't do what you tell me*, etching into my mind.

Be good.

I *was* good. I had never felt more alive.

It's now or never to make people notice you.

I finished my beer and took a few more swigs of my spirits. Without understanding how, the drive of the Rage-ing beat thrust me to my feet.

I danced. On my own.

And I didn't give a shit what anyone thought.

Alcohol.

Best wishes,
Me

I heard screaming. A lot of it. Mum.
    Footsteps. A lot of them. Mum and Demetri.
    The same words repeated. A lot. Mum.
    A high-pitched whine in self-defence. Once. Demetri.
    The screaming grew louder. And closer. Outside my bedroom door.
    I swung open my door.
    I didn't know what I was going to say, but it would be something, *any*thing, to stop the rage.
    I saw a knife. A serrated steak knife. In her hand, stretched out in front of her.
    Demetri turned his back, to flee down the hall, but she lunged forward and stabbed him in the back.
    I heard a sound, like a muted punch, and then a sharp inhale.
    Images of blood splatter and hospitals flicked through my mind.
    Of Mum being arrested for domestic violence.
    I thought it should be the other way around. Women didn't do these things.
    My overactive mind. The cut on his back was tiny.
    Mum had been weak.
    From Valium withdrawal.

My head throbbed. A siren wailed from the nearby fire station on Bell Street. At fifteen I still didn't step on the cracks in case I'd break my mother's back.

go

I reached our driveway, relief starting to kick in. Soon I could put my heavy school bag down, I thought, and lie in bed, take an Aspro, and stare at the ceiling for a couple of hours before dinner, which would probably be one of the following meals: vegetable pie, zucchini slice, omelette and salad, or spiral pasta with canned salmon. The chunks of vertebrae in the salmon always made me want to puke.

I opened the front door and let it slam shut. As I dragged my schoolbag to my bedroom, it whacked against the back of my legs with each step.

BANG! BANG! BANG!

It came from the kitchen. Mum was going through another drug-induced rage. I feared for her safety. But mostly I feared I'd be inconvenienced. Demetri was visiting his parents in Greece on his own.

Maybe she's taking her rage out on dinner?
Just ignore it.
But what if something's happened?
Do you really care? You don't need this shit.

I rolled my eyes and snuck to the kitchen door, thinking she might be swiping stuff out of the cupboards the way she used to swipe stuff off my bookshelves and then tell me to clean it up for no reason other than being mad. Once when that happened, a snow ball smashed into pieces and the liquid and fragments of glass were stuck in my carpet. Of course, being the most logical thing to do in my mind, I had grabbed the vacuum cleaner and sucked it all up. Which resulted in me breaking the vacuum cleaner. I can't remember whether I had been too old for the wooden spoon by then.

BANG! BANG! BANG!

The kitchen door was open just a crack. It was always

open just a crack. The door hadn't closed properly since Mum announced that the house had moved.

I peered through the gap, but couldn't see anything other than a shadow of movement reflecting on the glossy canary yellow cupboards.

Silence.

I was about to creep away and let her be when I heard a big long *moooaaaan*, and *BANG! BANG! BANG!*

My heart jumped into my throat and I pushed open the door to find Mum hitting herself over her head with a frying pan.

BANG! BANG! BANG!

"Muuuum!" I groped for the frying pan before it landed on her head one more time.

"The insects. They won't stop. What's happening to me?" Mum whispered like someone had their hands around her neck—shaking, pale, gaunt, eyes glazed over like the devil was controlling her movements.

She fell limp in my arms.

I trembled, terrified she had died, unable to comprehend what the hell had just happened.

What do I do? Call the ambulance? Demetri in Greece? Tony and Margaret?

Fuck her. She's breathing. She'll wake up on her own.

But what if she's dead?

She's not dead.

How do you know?

I don't remember what happened next. In my mind I left her, passed out on the kitchen floor. But I think I had stayed. My memory is so blurred I may have subconsciously blocked it out.

I don't remember anything but my bedroom ceiling.

And moaning.

There was always the moaning.

Mum's crazy behaviour was a result of cutting down on her Valium intake. She took the pills on and off depending on how 'good' she felt. This inconsistent pill popping meant she was in a constant state of Benzodiazepine withdrawal. Her moods fluctuated dramatically and without warning. We were all oblivious to the fact. The lack of literature available in the 90s about Benzodiazepines and their effects was startling. Unfortunately for Mum, she had to figure it all out on her own.

One similar night after school, I remember her sitting in her kitchen chair by the couch in the living room, towel still rolled up inside a Safeway bag to support her lower back, which she continued to believe was the crux of her health problems. We finished eating and started watching *The 7:30 Report* when Mum jumped out of her chair and bolted to the telephone in the corridor.

Mum paced left and right as far as the telephone cord would allow. She slammed the phone down and re-entered the living room.

"He's not answering." Mum pulled her fringe back so that it stretched the skin on her forehead. She wiped sweat from her upper lip and cupped her hand over her mouth.

Not again. Really? Why can't she just get a grip?

I don't know how to handle this. Please please please don't have another freak out. Please.

Just say what you have to say and get through it.

"Who's not answering?" I said, probably sounding bored and uncompassionate, when in actual fact, my heart was pounding in my ears. My stress, however, was surely triggered by the thought that *my* wellbeing would be in danger. Again.

"Demetri. What if something's happened to him?" Mum paced the width of the living room more times than I could count before she halted at the window to see if he might be miraculously strolling up our driveway all the way from Greece. She created a gap in the blinds to get a better view outside and squinted. The slat clicked like a castanet.

Mum moaned, paced the width of the room again, and stopped at the front door. She looked through the peep hole as if the view through that might alter what she saw outside.

"It's the morning there," she said. "He should be answering the phone."

"Maybe he's swimming," I said.

"It's winter!"

"Maybe he's getting the bread."

"Maybe he's dead!"

"What are you talking about?"

"What if he fell off his bike? Fell off a cliff? What if no-one even knows he's wounded and dying?"

Mum's voice grew louder and more frantic.

"I'm sure he's fine, Mum. Just call again in five minutes."

"How do you know? How do you know he's fine, Jessica?" Mum was screaming now, pacing faster, banging her fists on the walls, breathing erratically, pulling at her hair, her clothes, clutching her stomach, wiping tears from her cheeks as if they were made of thick black paint.

"I don't know what to do!"

"What do you mean?"

"I can't live on my own, Jessica. Look at me! I can't live on my own!"

"Mum, please. Just *calm* down." I didn't know what to

do to help her, to help control the panic. It was impossible to calm her down. Hopeless. Everything I said had no meaning to her when she was in this state. I might as well have recorded myself and pressed play every time we ended up in this situation. The best I could do for my own sanity—and I convinced myself that it was for my Mum's sanity too—was to act like nothing was wrong. But acting like nothing was wrong turned me into a cold heartless bitch with ice solid facial expressions that made my Mum think I hated her.

I loved her.

But not at the expense of feeling like crap.

So I would think about the panic attack being over and holing up in my bedroom with my Discman, listening to PJ Harvey and Nick Cave and The Tea Party and Babes in Toyland. Music that made my existence have meaning and no meaning at the same time. Music that would numb the ache in my chest, stomach, and head enough to almost feel empty.

Emptiness is what I thought I felt. Loneliness. Unlove. Invisible and redundant.

But in actual fact, I think I was so full of negative emotions that true emptiness might have been a relief.

"Jessica, help me! Oh my God, my scalp is going to burn off. *Please*, do something. Something. Anything!"

I stared at her in silence as she choked on her saliva.

When I didn't react, she whacked her head into the wall.

I jumped off the couch and ran to her side to try and pull her away from the wall.

"Mum. Please don't do this, *please*!"

I cried and hugged her. Her body shook in my arms, her silent sobbing trapped at the top of her throat.

I don't know whose arms hung rigid by their side. They were most likely Mum's, but they could have been mine too. I was trapped in a madhouse, unable to move. I couldn't breathe anymore. It was either find a way to die or get out. It sounds melodramatic, I know, but the combination of puberty and depression *is* melodramatic. And depression has a way of fluctuating to its peak without warning.

I thought about the possibility of moving out, but then I would have had to get a job, and I would have probably had to quit school, right when I was starting to feel I might make some friends.

I didn't want to do that. I didn't want to jeopardize the possibility of becoming 'cool' and showing the bullies what I was 'truly' made of.

There had to be another solution, I thought.

I soon found one without realizing I had.

part three
1996-1998

part three
1996–1998

go

When I write music, you make me ...

feel ambitious (unattainable), and motivated (I'll never manage it), and a need to be another person. (What do I have to give up?) You make me want to destroy my life as I know it. (Can I do it without anyone noticing?)

You always make me ...

debilitatingly depressed (I can't claw my way through city drains forever, man), jealous (of all the famous rock stars), feel like myself again (but the mirror doesn't reflect the right person), and cry (It's easier to write books—I can pretend the feelings are fictional.)

Why do you make me feel ...

Abandoned? (no-one really knows me) Empty? (my bones are brittle and dry and break into archaeological remains every day) Weak? (Have I wasted my life away on you?) Loveless (—).

Then you throw me into the clouds and make me feel ...

powerful (I could sing Madonna off the stage any day), rich (with desire and guilt and hunger), and alive (my head buzzing with Marshall's soothing hum).

But I know I'll always be ...

a phony (I'm sure I've been pretending I can play guitar all my life), unborn (only with my headphones on), and Jesus (crucified to misery).

You start with the same letter as Run.

Please spare me ...

the desperate need to run after you.

It was mid 1996 when the smell of a stranger's sheets stimulated my senses enough to wake me from inebriated oblivion. My school friends gathered round me, some with fingers over lips, others with open jaws, a few with dipped heads, muttering, whispering, laughing. Tim was there. But Nelly hadn't made it to Joe's party. She asked me, the next week at school, if I was okay. I said yes. I can't say if that was a lie.

"Jess!" Fae called, ran to my side and shook me, her long blonde hair tickling my cheek. I was still semi-passed out, but flashes of smashing my bottle of port in a bath tub, vomiting, muttering illogical ridiculousness, and then flirting with a guy nicknamed Buzz, reminded me how I got there. My breath quickened, my head pounded, and my stomach gurgled.

I looked down at my body in this strange bed. Nausea enveloping me like damp and mould.

I was stark naked and in desperate need to puke.

"Buzz. What did you do?" Tim whispered. The disgust in his voice travelled to the forefront of my earshot. I couldn't see him, but I heard Buzz scoff. I was so wasted that the room and my friends resembled a blurred and pixelated dreary-coloured mess.

"She wanted it," Buzz said. I heard a shoulder-shrug in his tone.

Fae sat me up and another girl with a lisp gathered my clothes. They helped me dress. One was laughing a bit, sarcastically, saying I was an idiot for letting this happen.

I was only fifteen.

Fifteen and no longer a virgin.

You've done it now. So fucking what?

Severe nausea overpowered the looming embarrassment I was sure to feel the next week at school.

Because of this day, twenty years ago at the time of writing this, I have never considered sex to be something special. Even now I struggle to give it meaning. I have to meditate. Prepare myself. Remind myself that it's *good*—

go

that it's not just an act of human nature that happens at random for no particular reason, that it can mean ... *love*. I *know* this. But sometimes, I just don't care. I could happily live the rest of my life without sex again.

And I'm only thirty-five.

This is a sad fact. But I have accepted it.

Somehow, once the girls had dressed me, I ended up in the bathroom again. I threw up some more and checked, on instinct, if I was bleeding. I'd heard a million times that you bled the first time, but there was nothing there. I wondered if I'd actually had sex before this night and couldn't remember.

A couple of hours later I was functional enough to call my mum, feign a convincing joyous tone of voice, and make her believe I'd only ingested one alcoholic drink and was having a great time. Because I had a huge problem. There was no way I was going home in that state. I looked like I'd been dipped in a bath of sugar syrup and pasted to the concrete.

Joe, with his funky freckles, pale skin, and ginger dreadlocks, hovered in front of me as I used his wireless house phone standing in the middle of his misty suburban street.

"I'd really like to stay late, the party is really fun, can I stay the night?" I gave Joe a silent thumbs up when he whispered if I was all right.

"I'd really prefer it if Demetri picked you up," Mum said.

"But it could go for ages still and I don't want you to have to stay up that late. Please can I just stay? It's all pretty easy-going. We're just dancing and having fun."

"All right. But please be careful. Don't drink too much."

"I won't, thanks!"

And then ...

I knew I could get away with anything.

"You want me to beat him up for ya?" Joe asked with a laugh as I handed him the phone. He looked at the ground with a smirk and kicked a couple of pebbles.

I shook my head, trying to tame the dizziness enough to get inside and horizontal.

I don't remember where I actually slept that night. I don't even remember hating Buzz for what he'd done.

To be fair, Buzz *was* one year younger than me. I'd flirted with him. I'd led him to the bedroom myself. Well ... I don't really remember that. It could have been him that led me. But that's what I tell myself. I tell myself I was a teenage idiot and I drove into the dark woods of my own free will.

It wouldn't be the last time I drove into the dark woods either. Every weekend, I'd total myself, not only to avoid dealing with the feelings my home life dredged up, but to be the person I wanted others to see.

The person I wanted others to see was mysterious and intriguing. A girl every guy wanted to get their hands on. I wanted to be the life of every party, just like mum was. I wanted to do the crazy shit my friends did so I would feel a part of the 'gang.' Above all, I wanted to be *liked*. I needed to be seen as being the cool girl, and I needed to be seen not caring what people thought of me (though I did, very much.) That was the key. Being *perceived as*. Whatever was left of me, beneath my skin, was no longer of any importance.

It was my reflection that mattered the most.

But even though my peers eventually 'liked' the weird and mysterious and kinda crazy-fun chick I'd eventually become, sacrificing the real me meant disliking myself.

And that gave me even more reason to run.

go

Siobhan backed me into my locker, told me I was beautiful, and thrust her tongue into my mouth. Her tongue ring clicked against my teeth as I scrunched her pink hair into my fist. We ground our groins together and groaned to a soundtrack of muttering and whispering students. I can only imagine what my black lipstick looked like smudged all over my face.

"Hey! Cut that *out* right now!" The vice principal stared at us from the end of the corridor before charging down and pulling us apart as if breaking up wrestlers.

The bell rang for recess. The vice principal glared, mute. Siobhan and I smiled at each other, smirked at the vice principal, and walked away in opposite directions.

We were now an item. That was the first time we had ever touched.

```
Wanna go out with me?
Yep.
Cool.
Let's kiss.
```

A couple of weeks later in assembly, our form teacher, Mr Wilson, blabbered on about our excursion to see the director's cut of Kenneth Branagh's *Hamlet*. I was in love with Shakespeare so I was excited. But I also fantasized about sneaking some more of my mother's vodka into a water bottle to take with me. I had it all planned out in my head: I could sit in the back of the cinema with Siobhan. She could touch me. I could touch her. We could both get pissed, and not care if we got caught.

We wouldn't get caught. Getting caught wasn't something we did.

As I sat in the assembly hall envisioning Siobhan and myself feeling each other up, I listened to Mr Wilson's voice turn into a muffled mess behind the visions of my daydreams. I wondered whether people really did stuff like that in cinemas, or whether it was just talk. Regardless, I thought it would be fun and daring, and entertained the idea until I found out Siobhan wasn't able to make it. It cost money that her mother couldn't afford—a mother I hardly ever saw, even when I stayed at her house.

"Lemon!" a kid called out, extending the vowels as some kind of insult. I would soon discover it was a derogatory term for 'lesbian.' I was knocked out of my trance when a lemon hit me in the back. Another almost hit Mr Wilson.

Mr Wilson sent the kid outside, but said nothing to me, nor did he tell the kid to apologize for the abuse.

At first I was grateful and pleased he recognized the kid was in the wrong, but then immediately realized he'd called him out on his behaviour due to it disrupting *him*.

It wasn't to help me at all.

Even the people I was supposed to respect and look up to, people who were supposed to shape and inspire and teach right from wrong, saw me as someone not worth the attention or support. At that age, bigotry was not something I was educated in, so this act was about *me* as a person. My sexuality was completely irrelevant.

That afternoon, when I went to Siobhan's house, she told me someone had left a bloody goat's head on her doorstep.

That's when alarm bells went off.

Was I a lesbian? But I had had sex with a guy, too. Did that mean I was bisexual?

Was this hostility and discrimination?

go

Not only was I not loved. I was now *hated*.

I sat on the edge of Siobhan's bed in silence and watched her write the lyrics of Hole's 'Miss World' on her white wall with permanent black marker.

I've made my bed, I'll lie in it ...

I hadn't paid much attention to Hole before this day, but suddenly, in these circumstances, their music resonated with me on a level music hadn't ever done so before. Courtney Love understood how it felt to be a teenage girl like me in the 90s: the self-loathing and shame that triggered constant thoughts of suicide, alongside the juxtaposing idea that we should be idolized and treated like queens. Teenage girls like me struggled with an overwhelming battle between hopelessness and piousness, the idea that looking 'cheap' would make others like us, that looking like a bruised and battered bum was cool, that we could drunkenly trip over our own feet until we bled from head to toe and still be perceived as beautiful and sexy.

I stared at myself in Siobhan's mirror as we listened to 'Doll Parts'—the lyrics conveniently narrating my own thoughts. My gelled and tattered-looking pixie hair was covered in glitter and infested with chunks of black rag and aluminium foil to hold random clumps of it together. My black lipstick starkly contrasted against my almost-white face, making me look like I was at the edge of death; the smudges of mascara on my cleavage made me look like I'd been in a bitch fight, and my too-short hot pants slipped over four layers of coloured ripped stockings screamed 'I'm a dyke slut.'

I whispered to myself in the mirror, *Someday, you will ache like I ache.*

I've spent my life believing I binged on alcohol because I was shy and it stripped me of inhibitions. But that's not entirely the truth, is it? The motivation came from you.

I didn't feel worthy of anyone's attention, and so you kept pushing—prodding—coaxing—me to get noticed. Even if I had to get drunk and make a fool of myself doing so.

Alcohol.

It gave me an excuse. For anything. Everything.

It gave me time out from you. From myself.

Are you proud?

Are you proud that you got me addicted to the attention? Are you proud that getting attention has become a form of escape from reality? Are you proud that even without alcohol, I have discovered other ways of feeling this sense of escape?

Now my alcohol is work.

Are you proud?

Every professional accomplishment is a chase after the spotlight so I do not feel I'm walking towards the edge of a burning flat earth. I need to be appreciated to rise from the depths of the unexplainable sadness and worthlessness you ingrained in me when I was bullied, when Demetri killed my ants, when Laurel died, and when my mother was always in so much pain it felt like the world revolved around her and my existence meant nothing.

Are you proud?

End of Year 10 Formal, at the Heidelberg Town Hall, hair slicked into a 1920s Eton crop. I wore a fluorescent orange body-fitted dress with an Elizabethan collar and black trimmings. A slit ran up to my hip, exposing my fish-net stockings and knee-high patent leather black platform boots. I was ready to make heads turn.

They did turn. But not in the way I had hoped.

Of course, I had my water bottle filled with a concoction from my parents' alcohol collection.

I sat at my table, when everyone else was out of their seats socializing, and took secret sips. The teachers had their eyes on me, though, I was sure. I was also sure they knew what was in the bottle. No-one spoke. Their suspicious expressions said it all.

I brought Siobhan as my date. I very soon became drunk. Of course. But it wasn't a happy drunk this time. I didn't want to get up and dance like I had done at Nelly's house; I wanted to curl up into a ball and hide. I had now transitioned from happy drunk to depressed drunk. There was always a point in my drunkenness, where, if I didn't keep drinking to keep the happiness going—which would eventually result in me throwing up in someone's bathroom, or in the street—I'd start feeling really low. So I'd just drink until it was impossible to feel anything other than complete whole-body numbness.

That numbness was worth every second of illness the next day.

That numbness was how I wished to feel all the time.

When it got closer to the end of the night, I was ready to go home and pass out in bed. But 'Tainted Love' started to play, and Siobhan dragged me onto the dance floor. Instead of dancing like one would to a funky tune, we *slow* danced.

I will not pretend I didn't feel self-conscious, but there was no way I was going to challenge her. I had to own this. I was the nutcase 'bisexual Nazi girl' (a nickname I was given after I had my head shaved) who liked to attract attention, and that's exactly the image I would maintain, even if the real me was trying to fight it.

To add fuel to the fire, we kissed in front of everyone.

This time we didn't get pulled apart, but I could hear the snarls and whispers of verbal abuse and feel their ogling eyes.

I smelt embarrassment oozing from teachers' pores. Some looked away, pretending not to notice, and others occupied themselves by rearranging the snacks on the table and collecting trash.

And that was enough to pull *me* apart.

No matter who I tried to be, it seemed there would always be someone who disliked me. Was I ever going to be accepted?

When I look back on moments like these, I wonder if I challenged people to like me, so I could purposely do something to make them uncomfortable and then blame them for it.

I felt like a phoney, and I didn't know how to fix it.

So my behaviour got worse.

At the Year 10 formal after party at a schoolmate's house, I smoked pot for the first time. I threw up violently. I had sex … with a boy. We dated for a week. Then I had sex … with another boy. I decided I'd fallen in love with him. He dumped me within a week because … I cheated on him with his best friend at another party. Then I moved onto another of his friends. He told me I was too special. That he wouldn't sleep with me when I was drunk. I decided that he was the one. He respected me, loved me. A week later, he chose another girl. A girl from another school I'd never met. He showed me a photo. She was pretty. I was jealous.

go

Siobhan and I soon grew apart. We still spoke often—whenever we'd run into each other at recess and lunch, and at any parties we both attended. Sometimes we'd have a drunken snog, and then move onto having a drunken snog with a different person within the next five minutes. And that was okay. I suppose we were both silently aware that our relationship was not serious, but exploratory.

I soon dove into a monogamous relationship. With a guy. One that didn't begin with sex. Interestingly, he was a cross-dresser. Again, in typical teenage fashion, we became an item in a matter of moments.

Tim: Frei likes you, but he's too shy to tell you.

Me: Oh okay.

Tim: Will you speak to him?

Me: Okay, where is he?

Tim: At the lockers.

Tim and I go to the lockers. Frei is waiting patiently. Tim and Frei had planned it.

Me: (to Frei) Tim says you have something to tell me.

Frei: Er ... yeah, I–I (chuckles) Do you, I don't know—I like you, I think you're cool.

Me: I think you're cool too.

(Actually, I hadn't even considered how I felt about him.)

Frei: Do you want to go out with me?

Me: Okay.

We walked to class holding hands.

Frei, in addition to dressing in women's clothing outside of school, liked to get high on cough syrup. Wherever he sat, he slumped over, as if he'd just injected himself with heroin. I knew this because I'd just seen *Trainspotting*. He was a tall and lanky Swede, with big brown puppy dog eyes and chocolate brown hair that shone and flopped like hair does in shampoo commercials. He wore it parted down the middle, and let it hang over his eyes.

After a few weeks of being together, we got shit-faced at his house with Tim and Nelly one Saturday night. Frei drank a bottle of cough syrup too quickly, threw up and semi-passed out. The three of us stood around him on his bed. His fishnet stockings were ripped, and the hairs on his legs were plastered onto his bony legs with sweat.

Tim said, "Frei, maybe you should get some help."

Frei groaned and told us to leave him alone. I didn't say a word, as I recognized so much of myself in Frei: the need to numb the pressure of the world and the self.

That Sunday evening at home, I wondered if anyone would ever tell *me* to get some help the next time I was catatonic on a stranger's front lawn. Or maybe people just didn't care if I got any help or not. It was raining outside that Sunday—an uncharacteristically tropical summer was creeping up on us.

Our front lawn was covered in plane tree leaves. I sat on my bed and stared out the window, noticing my reflection in the glass, my mind flitting from menial/irrational thought to menial/irrational thought ...

I'll be asked to rake the leaves up.

You won't be here. I don't know where you'll be, but you won't be here.

I could kill myself. I hate my bed sheets.

Pink and flowers are not you anymore.

I want black ones. Satin. I'll get a job. Buy some.

What's the point, you won't be here.

But I want to go to The Big Day Out. I'll wait to kill myself until after that.

But Mum won't give you money for a ticket.

go

I'll get a job and buy one myself.
You just wanna play music.
Mum's gonna ask me to wash the dishes in a minute.
Can't she just fucking do them herself?
Can't play music if I'm dead.
Can't go to The Big Day Out either.
Better not die. Yet. Or maybe.
Fuck it.

I wrote a new song that night about suicide. The lyrics sucked.

I wanted to be a rock star. But what was the point, I wouldn't be there, right?

I pressed play on my portable CD player, skipped straight to track four. 'Sweet '69' by Babes in Toyland. Played it a few times, then skipped back to track one, 'Hello.' Played it a few times, over and over, as the grey and the clouds and the rain and the broken driveway and crooked red letter box and the tufts of grass sticking through the cracks, the rain getting heavier, stronger, louder, a bottle-green garbage bin skidding down the road, it was flooding, the street was flooding, and I wanted to lie in it.

I've made my bed, I'll die in it. Courtney. Love. You. Frei. Siobhan, too.

But it didn't matter. I wouldn't be there. The next day, it would all be over. Fuck The Big Day Out. The likelihood of going was nil.

I didn't do it. (Obviously.)

I spent every day for months, pining for the weekend. And if there was no party to go to, I'd spend it locked up in my room, thinking of possible ways to kill myself that weren't going to cause me any pain.

I could have taken Mum's pills, but what if someone

found me before I died? Rushed me to the hospital and pumped my stomach? Then life would have been even worse, with all the counselling, and having to live with being a failure at the only thing that could have eventually given my overactive mind some peace.

I could have shot myself, but where would I have gotten a gun? And what if I survived that and ended up a vegetable, conscious of every single moment?

I could have slit my wrists, but that scared the hell out of me. All that pain and blood. No way. I couldn't cast myself in a horror movie.

So I tried to drown myself in the bath tub.

I couldn't hold my breath for more than a minute.

Lyrics to 'The Dark,' the first song I wrote in 1997:

The dark, I sit so quietly
the dark, I cry, loose between my knees
my lips tremble as I speak
wet with tears and shudders

Loose ends, drip off my face
loose ends, slide from my hips
life like, I slip away
I fall through, the hole in my face

It was a morning after I'd partied hard. I was supposed to get up and spend some time that Sunday doing some chores around the house.

But I was hung over, so I slept in. The blinds were shut, my door was shut. Mum's footsteps grew louder and heavier in the hallway, and the light that crept through the crack below my door flickered every time she passed.

Knock, knock. "Jess, get up. I can't wait all day."

I groaned and rolled over. Ignored her.

Knock, knock, knock. "Jess, I mean it. It's midday. Get up. Now."

"Soon," I mumbled. I went back to sleep.

Bang, bang, bang! "Get up right now or I'll get you up," Mum yelled.

She sounded frantic. I thought I'd better get up before the shit hit the fan. Just as I was about to push the covers off and crawl out of bed, Mum flung my door open, grabbed me by the hair, dragged me out of my bed and outside my bedroom door.

I clutched at my head and screamed as the pain shot through my scalp and down my neck.

"Muuuuuuum! Stoooooop!"

When she let go, I burst into tears, gasped for air, heaved and sobbed and crawled back into my room, slammed the door and leaned my back against it.

Where was Demetri?

I cried for so long and so heavily my head felt like a bowling ball balancing on a chop stick.

What have I done to deserve this?

What have you done? Nothing. She's a bitch.

I hate you, Mum. I hate you!

I don't remember her coming back for me. I don't remember anything but wanting to run. To run and hide as far away as possible.

And to never look back.

The only thing that prevented me from taking suicide one hundred per cent seriously was music.

In early 1997, my second-to-last year of high school,

I stepped in front of the red velvet curtain of the then renamed Macleod College with my twelve-string guitar. It was the annual let's-show-off-our-talented-students concert. I sat my rattling soon-to-be 'sweet' sixteen body in a classroom chair which had been placed at the edge of the stage just for me. Katherine, a girl I'd formed a duet with, followed with her violin, her blonde waist-length waves caressing her shoulders and glimmering in the stage lights. We exchanged nervous smiles as we quickly tuned our instruments amongst the quiet shuffling of feet and legs, the throat clearings, and echoing whispers coming from the audience.

I adjusted the position of the microphone, pinched the plectrum between my lips, and wiped sweat from my right hand onto my thigh. I was always nervous about it slipping out of my fingers and falling into the sound hole. Strumming bar chords on an acoustic guitar—especially a twelve-string—with bare fingers was painful. When it happened, I'd often rip the cuticles off my fingernails and bleed.

Being too nervous to introduce our duet to the audience of fellow students and parents, I gave Katherine a sideways glance, a curt nod, and launched straight into strumming PJ Harvey's 'Send His Love to Me.'

... *Send* Her *Love to Me* ...

The acoustics in the school gymnasium made it hard to hear clearly. My legs shook, making the guitar shake too. The shaking multiplied and travelled through every limb, even into my tongue, causing a level of vibrato I could never manage on my own when I tried. A couple of times, I knocked my front teeth onto the microphone, and Katherine missed a note, or played flat. But I didn't care.

All I could think about the whole time was whether Mum had made it.

She said she might not.

I hoped she would. But knew deep down the likelihood was pretty low. She wouldn't have said anything if she'd intended on coming. Despite that, it didn't make the disappointment of her not turning up any less hurtful.

All I wanted was Mum to be proud of me. To show her that giving me her guitar was a great thing.

Yes, I hated her sometimes.

But that hate was fuelled by love. A love so loyal, that I believe, as a teenager, I could not recognize it for what it really was. To me it was too much to handle, so I chose to show nothing because it was easier that way.

As Katherine and I drew out the final note of the song, the audience applauded and a few people whistled. I peered into the crowd to search for Mum. But she'd sent Tony as her stand-in.

There sat my two fathers. Clapping. Smiling. Proud.

Why do I always dream about the consequences of my death?

Sometimes everyone I've ever met in my entire life is at my funeral. They all sit in silence, as if judging me in jest, smirking at my photograph. It's in a metallic black frame propped up at the front of some church I never knew existed, on a cheap looking coffin.

Most times the only person by my coffin is my mother, with Serafeim, sitting somewhere in the background. Sometimes it's the opposite, with my mother in the background, and Serafeim at my coffin.

No-one ever cries. But I cry watching them from the sidelines. Never from above. Maybe when I die I'll be one of those ghosts that coexist with life, but never get seen. Notice any clues there? Do I still feel like I'm never noticed?

Tony and Demetri are never at my funerals. Ever. Not once.

Maybe they're hanging in the background somewhere, jamming on their guitars in silence, and I just can't see them. Or maybe I'm ignoring them. Sometimes I feel like my fathers don't think about me much. But it's most likely that I have neglected to think about them as often as I should.

I feel bad about that.

My mother and Serafeim have always come first. They're the ones I always want to tell my news to before anyone else. Now, they are also the first to dismiss the things important to me. "I'll read/look/listen to it later," or "It's hard for me to read, you know that, my eyesight is too bad," are the most common things I hear from them. But I still persist. And I don't blame them for dismissing me. They have lives too. I'm not the only person on this planet. And still, they are the first people I turn to, no matter what. Even when I know they're going to say no. Even when I know they're not 'noticing' me. Progress perhaps?

Maybe that's why they are always at my funeral.

Because I'm not running from them anymore.

In March of 1996, Hard Candy released a single called 'Junior.' In early to mid 1997, when my parents were getting ready to film the video clip for it (because they couldn't afford to make it sooner than that), Mum came into my room and asked if she could borrow one of my dresses. It was a daring dress I'd bought in Greece that would always turn heads—a bright orange, yellow, and white-striped mini with text on the front that said "Kick

go

It Out." I can't count the times I wished Mum would see me in that dress and get the message.

Of course, I said she could borrow it. But I hated her for it. It was almost as if she was stealing a part of my identity and individuality and making it her own. Despite her having hosted the best sixteenth birthday party ever, in which I played a mini gig in our backyard, I remember thinking, hasn't she taken enough from me?

Wearing my dress was wearing my identity. The identity I'd been building to separate myself from her. And now she wanted to mix us up again.

I punished Mum for this. By continually being cold, mean, and unresponsive when she asked for my help. When I listen to the lyrics of 'Junior,' I wonder whether the song was written as a letter to me. Every time I hear this song, it brings me to tears because it really shows how alone and insignificant my mother must have felt. And somehow, I think she saw I was feeling something similar. The mix of rage, sadness, and helplessness is prominent, yet cleverly hidden behind the chilled bluesy groove of the bass and drums, tricking listeners into wanting to get up and move. But whenever I listen ... whenever I *really* listen, I understand that the song is about my mother and me: two pulverized hearts and minds struggling to live with demons and doing everything possible to hide them in a pretty neat package.

```
JUNIOR

Had a little accident,
Nearly shot you dead.
And it's so cold in the winter here,
When the storm clouds fill the black around your head.
From the window
```

jessica bell

```
Sometimes I can only see myself
The reflection to be so cold and deceptive
through the eyes of someone else
So Junior
You want more
More than your head can hold
More than a dinosaur
Yeah, Junior
Watch me speed
at the end of this open road
you could jump like me

Nothing falls like darkness
when it falls all over me
and falls all over you
and the world too
And you're nothing but a shadow
in the corner of this darkened road

Curl yourself
into these arms
I'll be your only girl
Let me try to catch these foolish words
as you spit them at this ugly world
senses as sharp as razor blades
fall all over me, yeah
but I don't feel so old and as cold as you
sometimes appear to be
```

The video clip[10] to this song was their last before Mum's situation escalated to a point of sheer physical and

---

10 You can watch the 'Junior' video clip on YouTube here: *bit.ly/HardCandyAU2*

go

emotional agony and desperation. She couldn't keep up with the rock 'n' roll lifestyle without the drugs and alcohol, but she couldn't keep *living* with the drugs and alcohol. It all had to stop. It wasn't more than a year later when the band broke up, and my parents decided to look into selling the house and moving to Ithaca for good so she could get completely clean.

But before that, 1997 got worse.

Every couple of months, I'd try to find a new way to do my hair—a new way to be considered a freak. Something that would make me look weird*er* than I already presented myself. Something that would make everybody stare. I needed to give them a reason to stare as though I had a disease. I hated being looked at from kids outside of my peer group. If I could distract them with something superficial, I didn't have to focus on the reasons I was weird inside either. My heart, my mind, my soul. They were even weird to me. Trying to understand myself was a challenge. I could hardly expect shallow-minded selfish dipshits, who were my 'schoolmates,' to figure me out if I couldn't do it myself.

One day after school, I got straight into the shower. I had a headache. Again. I leaned my forehead against the pink and white tiled shower wall. Hot water cascaded down my neck and back, steam filling the bathroom despite the fan. I liked the water hot. Really hot. Those few blissful minutes under the running water washed away the emotional exhaustion and struggle that would multiply as each day progressed.

I lathered my now short bleach-blonde hair with Sunsilk and rinsed it out, careful not to get it in my eyes.

Flecks of silver glitter were stuck to my hands and not washing off. I knew Mum would have a go at me later for leaving it all over the house (even if it wasn't) if I didn't remove all evidence of it from my body. My breasts hurt and I had cramps. All I wanted to do was curl up in bed and dream of being a rock star and showing all the fuckheads at school that I was so much better than them.

The bathroom door flung open and hit the steel stool behind it. *WHACK!*

"What the fuck did you do? You fucking broke it!" Mum yelled, and immediately left again, slamming the door behind her. I stood there, frozen under the running water. It was turning cold, but there was no way I was getting out now.

Mum came back, flinging the door open even harder this time, yelling something about me not respecting her music equipment and I was never to touch her microphone again.

WHACK! Once more she slammed the door, her raging footsteps along the floorboards echoing through the house. I was still frozen in position, fear and loathing multiplying in my stomach so fast I wanted to vomit. I remember thinking I hadn't touched her microphone for over a week and she'd used it since then, but there was no way I was going to tell her that.

In she came again, bringing with her a list of irrational insults I'd heard a million and one times, yelling at me so loud that her breath parted the steam.

"It wasn't me. I didn't do anything to your microphone." I think I was whispering, but I'm sure I was yelling in my head. I knew that back-talk would aggravate her more, so I had gotten used to being silent. But the silence was beginning to have consequences too. Her Valium withdrawal-induced rages were getting bigger, louder, and more frantic. I could put up with being slapped, and even dragged along the floor by my hair, but since that day with the attempted steak knife stabbing, I was always scared of what she was capable of.

"Stop lying, you're a fucking liar! Get out! Get out of the fucking shower you selfish little bitch. You're punished. Two months." She left, slamming the door again.

The water was running cold now, and I shivered. Mum barged back in, pushing the door even harder this time. I thought I heard something crack. She just stared at me, her nostrils flaring, her previous words booming over and over in my head. *You selfish little bitch, you selfish little bitch*. She slammed the door. Again. And then for, I suppose good measure, she decided she wanted to make more noise, and slammed the door once more without saying anything to me.

What followed were a string of expletives I couldn't recognize and a howling so long and abnormal, I thought her head was going to explode, smoke, and whistle. She paced up and down the corridor a few times, moaning, until I heard Demetri's voice, calm, but a little high-pitched, as that's what often happened when he felt challenged.

"Erika. Erika. Stop. Show me."

Next I heard a deep guttural cry. The bathroom door swung open again, but this time, all she did was show her bloody hand, with the top of her middle finger hanging from the knuckle by a thread of skin.

I dry-wretched.

My heart beat so fast I couldn't recognize the difference between the thumping of my own distress and my parents' erratic footsteps and frantic voices.

Demetri called something out to me, the front door opened and closed, and then there was ...
silence.

I took a deep shaky breath and turned the taps off. Shivering, I slid open the glass door of the shower, stepped onto the mat, and wrapped a towel around myself. Blood started trickling down my leg. I cleaned myself up, got dressed, and finally let the tears break free.

I was alone. I was allowed to cry.

When I stepped out of the bathroom, I saw blood splattered all over the corridor walls. With my breath caught in my throat, I stared, but only for a brief moment, before pulling myself together. I grabbed a sponge from the kitchen, and scrubbed it all away.

When I'd finished, I sat in the living room and watched TV, waiting for my parents to come home.

I didn't wonder whether Mum was all right.

Why does she keep doing this to me?
You have done nothing to deserve this.
Bitch. Fucking bitch.

Mum sat in her kitchen chair, in the middle of the living room. She stared towards the window looking to the front lawn, but her glazed and hazy eyes were facing the wall just to the left of it. Her skin was cold and smelled toxic. Her arm hung bandaged in a sling. The surgeon had managed to sew her finger back on, but he'd also pumped her full of drugs. The drugs she was trying to quit.

Bruises yellowed one side of her face and under one eye. Demetri told me the hospital staff assumed he'd beaten her up, but she'd actually fainted when stepping out of the Beetle and whacked her face on the passenger door as she collapsed.

go

There she sat. Day and night. For what I remember as weeks. Staring at the wall. It was as if she was a vegetable. She'd rarely move from this position. Demetri and I had to help her shower, to go to the toilet, to force her to eat. As she'd go through the motions of normal everyday routines, she'd moan and cry and whimper. Every utterance would sound like she was being physically tortured. She was afraid of water because it felt like needles piercing her skin. Everything tasted like metal, she said. Her head was infested with insects. Footsteps sounded like thunder. Clinking dishes like cracks of lightning. If Demetri was late home by even one second, it meant he'd been in a car accident, or murdered, and her panic attacks were so loud and fierce I feared she'd accidentally kill herself.

Or purposely kill herself.

But her occasional catatonic states were the scariest. There were times she wouldn't respond when I spoke to her, even though her eyes were wide open. And times she wouldn't wake up when I shook her. I sat and watched. Every time. Every time I watched. I watched. I watched my mother suffer through agonizing physical and mental pain. And I hated her for it. I hated my own mother. And I hated myself for hating my mother.

It would be better if she just died.
I don't want my mother to die!
Yes. You do.
I don't. I don't!
You don't love her.
I LOVE HER. I don't. I do. I hate her. I don't.

She soon grew gaunt and grey-skinned and frail. I don't remember helping her much. And when I did, I pretended I was elsewhere. I resented her for doing this to *me*. Her involuntary drug addiction, her withdrawal, was happening to *me*. I wanted to run away. To never have to come home from school and deal with a suffering psycho ever again. But I hated her for something she couldn't control. It wasn't as if she'd chosen to abuse drugs. She was prescribed them for a back problem—a phantom back pain caused by drug withdrawal from other prescribed drugs to begin with, but what doctor in those days would admit to such a thing? She had become so used to the high dosage of Valium and Brufen that she said she was able to simultaneously consume an entire bottle of Vodka before a gig, and feel *normal*.

I honestly can't believe she never died of an overdose.

Looking back, every time she called me a 'selfish little bitch,' she was probably right. But each time those words were uttered, I would hurt so deep inside that I don't think I even realized it was pain. And because I bottled it up. It became anger and hatred. So I let that out on my mother. Silently. For years. Because I numbed myself. I was protected.

I realize now that all I wanted was Mum to love me. To not be lost in space for once when I spoke to her. To not feign interest when I wanted to share some school work with her. To not fear that every innocent word I uttered might be construed as an insult and result in rage. To not be caught in the storm of her panic attacks feeling helpless, frightened, insecure. Essentially, I felt like I was dealing with this on my own. Demetri offered no support to me. How could he? He seemed to be dealing with this in his own way too. By simply getting on with it ... in silence. Every night after work, he'd come home, cook dinner, wash the dishes, close himself in the music room and drown his sorrows in guitar solos.

But can you imagine the frustration and sadness and feeling of abandonment that must have caused my mother? To have two people, who were supposed to love her the most, staring at her with cold blank faces whenever she needed help, and disappearing behind closed doors every chance they got so they didn't have to deal with the pain it caused *them*?

We weren't the ones *suffering*. My mother was.

The memories make my stomach churn.

Years later, in my early twenties, when my love-hate relationship with my mother had reached its final tether, when she had become relatively well again, and completely drug-free, I exploded. I told her what a horrible mother she was, how she'd bullied me and destroyed me, that she was the reason I was always so depressed, how she'd left me with emotional wounds that scarred unevenly, how self-centred and cruel she was, how alone and unloved she'd made me feel ...

She burst into tears, and threw the exact same words back at me.

She was absolutely right.

I still wanted a ticket to the Big Day Out, a massive music festival that was held in five Australian cities annually. I'd missed out on getting one for January 1997, so my goal was to get one for 1998. But my parents still couldn't afford it. So I got a weekend job at a pharmacy (oh, the irony!) in Greensborough, just a couple of train stops from my school.

I'd get changed into a navy blue smock in a room the size of a closet.

I had to clock in and clock out of my twenty-minute lunch break, and one five-minute tea break, so that I wouldn't get paid for the time I sat in the room the size of a closet, shovelling food and tea down my throat as fast as I possibly could.

There was no small talk. Just stocking shelves and hidden medicine cabinets and serving customers. If I spoke about anything non-work-related, I'd be told to "not utilize working hours to socialize, please."

If I made a mistake with the register, it got docked from my pay.

The pharmacist was a moderately built twenty-five-year-old white male with a politician's haircut. Every Saturday morning he'd talk himself up in the room the size of the closet: "You are the man. The ladies love you. You're too sexy." One time he added "for your t-shirt."

He made me remove my nose ring. I resented him for it.

I didn't steal any meds.

But I did earn enough money to buy that Big Day Out ticket. It was the first thing I'd ever saved up for with my own money, and I was proud of myself. But along with the good always comes the bad: I got fired for not smiling at customers.

I told my parents that I'd quit.

Demetri knocked on my bedroom door so quietly I could hardly hear it. I turned off The Tea Party's 'Transmission' and he opened the door an inch.

"Mum wants to speak to you," he said, reluctant to enter. He puckered his brow and cleared his throat.

My stomach sunk like it always did when I thought I'd done something wrong.

You'll deal with it.

It'll be irrational.

Maybe you'll be lucky and it will pass as quickly as it comes.

go

It never passed as quickly as it came, but for some reason the hope was always at the back of my mind, as if I had accepted my mum's rage wasn't real, wasn't *her*, just the drugs speaking. Of course, in my mind I knew this, but trying to convince my heart was a struggle.

I entered the living room. Cigarette smoke and flecks of dust floated in a ray of sunshine beaming through the slits of the blinds. I walked through it, imagining it was fairy dust, my innocence still finding excuses to outshine my demons. Mum had migrated from a kitchen chair to the couch—progress—but still using the rolled-up towel in a Safeway bag to support her back. In her trembling hands was one of many letters.

Love letters that were written to me by Siobhan. They were over a year old and we were now just friends.

"Can you explain this?" Mum said, trying to swallow her rage.

I hadn't confided in any of my family about Siobhan. It was private. Plus, I didn't even know if that's what I *was*, or whether it was just 'sexual experimentation' as the adults liked to call it.

I couldn't say anything. Totally tongue-tied. I didn't even know what I was in order to give it a name. Was I really bisexual? Or just messing about?

A sound escaped my mouth, but I was interrupted before I managed to form any words.

"How could you lie to me like this?" Mum said.

Tears welled up in my eyes; the living room grew small and claustrophobic. I wanted to get out of there and run to where nobody knew me and therefore had nothing to judge. And it was a hundred times worse that this judgment was coming from someone who was meant to love me unconditionally.

I didn't know what to say, except, "I didn't lie."

I think I started crying. I'm not sure. I'm not even sure if Mum's voice was raised. Any words that came out of her mouth in those days were all the same: scary. I had long learnt how to block them out, turn her voice into background noise, into numbness. Words without consonants. Sentences without intonation.

She was a mouth without a face.

"What's wrong with having private things?" I finally mustered the courage to ask, holding back a torrent of tears and anger. I wanted to yell. I didn't. I knew it would cause a hurricane.

"I won't tolerate you two-timing. It's not right."

I laughed. I think. Or maybe I just did inside. I couldn't believe she would just assume I was doing that.

"You're seeing Frei. *And* you're seeing Siobhan?" she wiped a tear I could not see from below the rim of her brown-framed glasses.

"No! We're just friends."

"But what about this?" Mum whacked the pile of letters into her lap.

"It's from ages ago. We're not together anymore."

Silence.

Demetri tip-toed around behind me. Standing there in support of Mum. I had no idea if he agreed with her. He never stuck up for me. Ever. He didn't even stick up for himself. Sometimes I wondered if he even knew how to speak out about the things he believed in at all.

Siobhan's letters disappeared. I didn't know how, or where to. I couldn't focus on anything except avoiding being thrown out. After the experience at the pharmacy, I knew I wasn't ready to make a go of it on my own. If being a responsible adult meant having a job like that, I didn't want any of it. At that moment, I thought that committing suicide might end up being my only option.

go

So I stood there, with my hands behind my back. Like I was being interrogated by a nun. My mother's lifestyle couldn't have been further from that of a nun. I didn't understand why this was such a big deal, especially when she was the type of woman to walk around at a party flashing her boobs, putting condoms on carrots, and sticking her finger up at the camera.

Maybe the rage came from a fear of losing me. Being so far removed from who I had become. My umbilical cord had been well and truly severed. I suppose Mum was feeling a great sense of loss, and the only way she knew how to express that was through anger.

"If I find out you're still seeing Siobhan—"

"I'm not."

The conversation was over.

My chest tightened. I wanted my Mum, but I couldn't have her. At least not the way I wanted her to be. Where had the mother gone that avenged my bullies and left my bedroom door open a crack so that I wouldn't be afraid of the Heidel monsters?

I missed her.

I missed her like hell.

But there was no way I was going to show it.

In early spring of 1997, on a Friday night in Edinburgh Gardens in North Fitzroy, I got plastered on cheap cask wine (consumed directly from the box by tilting my head back) with Nelly, Tim, Frei, and a few other school friends that were a part of the grungy crowd. (In my mind, there seemed to be five kinds of student at Macleod College: Grungy/Alternative, Artsy/Intellectual, Sporty Jocks, Popular Mean Girls, and Outright Thugs.)

We wandered as far from the main road as possible

without it disappearing from view so that random cops had less of a chance to see us, and sat in the middle of the grass, drinking as fast as we could. Others smoked pot—something I chose to avoid doing—but I stuck with cigarettes bummed off my friends because there was no way I was going to buy a packet for myself and have Mum find it. I have no idea how we got a hold of the booze. I'm assuming we all chipped in money and someone's parents bought the alcohol for us. Or one of us had a fake ID. I never actually remember buying alcohol myself.

It wasn't long before I was shit-faced. The wind whistled through the elm trees and I shivered as the temperature dropped. The rumble of traffic bellowed like a warning. And when I looked up from my kaleidoscopic lap, Demetri's white Beetle inched along the curb by the edge of the park.

I rolled my eyes, grabbed my bag, and realized my breath stunk. Demetri was five minutes early. Every minute away from home was important to me, so a mere five minutes early might as well have been a half an hour in my mind.

"Has anyone got any chewy?" I wobbled to my feet.

"Yeah, man," Nelly said, exhaling smoke as she passed her now-way-too-small-to-hold spliff to Tim. She rummaged through her dirty beige hemp backpack, pulled out a yellow stick of P.K. gum and popped a couple pellets into my hand. I shoved them in my mouth quickly and glanced towards the Beetle. Demetri stepped out of the car and waved his arms about as though I hadn't seen him. I waved back with a groan to signify I was coming.

Frei lay flat on his back with a thump and smudged his red lipstick all over his face.

"I'm so fucked. I'm sinking into the ground," he said.

go

I wondered whether to bend down and give him a kiss goodbye. I didn't.

"Seeya Monday." I pushed the chewy around my mouth to try and eradicate the stink of grog as much as possible. I walked to the Beetle, making a conscious effort to step in a straight line. The ground swayed under my feet as I tried to steady my loose and heavy body.

It was time to smile and sound jolly. To fool Demetri into thinking I'd had a wonderful social experience, but also make a point of how tired I was, too, especially seeing as I'd been at school all day, so that I could go to bed and stop pretending the world wasn't spinning a hundred kilometres an hour around my head.

But when I got to the car, Mum was in the passenger seat. Something I hadn't expected. It was usually only Demetri, and he was either gullible or too afraid to say anything. My heart picked up speed. Mum stepped out and pulled the front seat forward. I looked at the ground in case my eyes were red.

"You have a good time?" she asked, ducking slightly to try for a glimpse of my face.

Without looking up, I stepped into the back and said, "Yeah, it was great fun," in my happiest voice possible. I feared I had spoken too loudly. I couldn't tell whether I *actually* spoke loud or whether it had only seemed that way in my head.

"Are you drunk?" There was no beating around the bush with my mother.

"No." I said. "Of course not. It was just, you know, a picnic."

Demetri turned the key in the ignition and the Beetle chugged into motion. I looked out the window, still avoiding eye contact. Mum glared at me through the rear-view mirror.

"What did you do?" she asked. I stupidly turned to face forward and before I could answer, she accused me of lying.

"I'm not drunk. I'm just tired." I noticed a waver in my voice.

"If you're not drunk, then why are you chewing gum?"

Silence.

The beat of my heart gained speed, the blood gushed straight to my head, and my face grew hot.

You're an idiot! You hate chewing gum!

What was I supposed to do? I had to do something.

She didn't even ask to smell your breath. You could have gotten away with it.

Well how was I supposed to know?

Fuck. You're screwed.

I know. She'll punish me.

I think she'll do more than that.

Bitch.

Mum and Demetri whispered to each other for the remainder of the trip home. Despite being caught, I still pretended to look sober—whether I was successful or not I'll never know. But my reflection wasn't having any of it.

Bitch. You should spit in her face.

Fucking bitch. Who is she to talk? Who is she to fucking talk?

Bitch.

You call me a selfish fucking bitch? What about your fucking double standards?

Bitch.

When we got home, Mum made me stand in the doorway of my bedroom. She stood in front of me and squinted—a laser stare directly through my pupils. Demetri stood next to her with his arms crossed and head tilted to the

go

side. I remember thinking he looked like he was posing for a band photograph.

I stared at Mum with a scathing smirk on my face. "What?" I snapped.

Mum scoffed. "What do you think you're doing?"

I craned my neck. "What do I think *I'm* doing? What do you think *you're* doing?" Everything was spinning. All I wanted to do was lie down, but there was no way I was going to let that on. I kept saying to myself to push through. To not let them get the upper hand.

"What do you mean by that?" Mum said.

"You've got double standards," I slurred. There was no stopping the effects of the wine now.

Mum's eyes widened and she took a small step back. It looked like she was about to cry. Then she stepped forward again and poked me in the chest. I stumbled backwards but regained composure by leaning all my weight into the left of the door frame.

"I'm *sick*." The word 'sick' snaked through Mum's lips with revulsion.

I didn't have a retort, so I just stared.

She spoke words. Words that became a muffled mess in my subconscious as I visualized punching her in the face, packing a bag, and running away for good. I could stay with Siobhan. Her parents never cared where she was or what she was up to. For sure she'd be able to help.

But there was one thing that sucked me back to reality.

"You're grounded."

Yeah, yeah, so what.

What's gonna happen?

No TV, no parties for a couple of weeks?

Who gives a fuck.

Perfect time to kill yourself.

"For two months. And no Big Day Out."

"What?" I said. "But I paid for that myself!"

"Not my problem." Mum ripped the ticket in half, and then in half again. She let the pieces drop to the floor and walked into the living room, slamming the door behind her. I can only imagine the tears she shed.

I was left standing there with Demetri.

"I'm very disappointed in you, Jess. I thought you were more sensible than this." He sighed and followed Mum.

I went to bed without taking my makeup off, and entertained the idea of running away, visualizing the confrontation I'd have in the morning when I walked out the door, over and over and over in my head. In one version, I snuck out the back door so I wouldn't be seen. In another version, I walked out the front door, straight past my parents without a word, and watched them run after me, crying, and physically trying to hold me back.

That won't work. You won't get away like that. You have to do it without being seen.

The next morning when I woke up, I ignored my queasy stomach and black eye-liner smudged all over my face, and packed a bag.

I'd intended to sneak out the back door to avoid passing my parents who were talking in the living room, but for once in my life, I chose not to hide.

That decision was not a step in the right direction psychologically. I'm sure I did it because I secretly wanted to be stopped.

"I'm leaving," I said, as I stepped into the living room. "For good."

Demetri tried to speak, but Mum interrupted him. "And where do you think you're going to go?"

"None of your business." I had no idea where I was going to go.

go

"If you walk out that door, that's it. I mean it," she said with a scowl, crossing her arms. "Don't ever think about coming back, you hear me?"

I puckered my brow and scoffed. Her cold words made my heart burn with rage, but I had to show I couldn't care less.

"Fine," I whispered, and shrugged.

I opened the door, slammed it shut behind me, and walked so damn fast up Bell Street towards Heidelberg train station that my knees could have touched the concrete before my feet.

I was outta there. But instead of celebrating, I burst into tears. I vomited a little in my mouth, and swallowed the bile-tasting liquid back down.

I did it.

You did it!

But I had no idea where I was going to go, or how the twenty bucks in my pocket was going to last me until I found a job.

I didn't make it any farther than Studley Road before Demetri pulled up beside me. I was about to enter the tunnel that led to the platforms at Heidelberg train station when he leaned over the passenger seat and swung open the door.

"Don't be stupid. Get in."

"Why?" I snapped.

Demetri rolled his eyes and tsked. "You know she doesn't mean it."

"Maybe she should think before she speaks." A pang of disappointment caused me to pause. Why did she have to be so mean? I just didn't understand it.

"Just get in the car, Jess."

Back at home, Mum was bawling her eyes out in the kitchen, pacing up and down the room like she often did when she was in pain because it hurt too much to sit. I thought that maybe she would show some compassion, that maybe she had realized what a bitch she was being and was about to grant me my Big Day Out ticket back.

She wiped her eyes, and lit a cigarette. She stared out the window and took a big long drag, making her look like a corpse as she sucked her cheeks in.

"Now I know why your grades are slipping," she said, holding her cigarette in the air and exhaling quickly so she could continue her lecture. "I really thought you were just a slow learner, that your teachers were overreacting. I'd had my suspicions—you think I don't know when you've been drinking?—but I had put it all down to you just being a teenager. But it's got to stop. Now. This binge drinking. Otherwise you're going to ruin your life."

"I'm not binge drinking." I rolled my eyes.

"You're sick every weekend. How is that not binge drinking? You really think I'm fooled by this 'I'm tired' bullshit?"

I shrugged. I thought it had been working well. I guessed not.

Mum took another drag, flicked ash into the sink, licked her lips and took a drag again.

"Have you had sex?"

"No!" I cried.

She glared at me. "Look me in the eye and tell me that you haven't."

I looked her in the eye without wavering. "I haven't had sex."

We held eye contact for what seemed like minutes before she took one last long drag from her cigarette.

"Okay," she said, taking a deep breath. "Well, I think it might be better for all of us if you went to live with Tony."

"What? No!"

I couldn't go to live with Tony. He'd moved to Townsville, Queensland, a completely different state. I'd lose contact with all my friends, have to make new ones, after all this effort I'd put in to being accepted. I couldn't handle starting my life all over again.

I burst into tears.

"I don't want to live with Tony. *Please* don't make me live with Tony. *Please!*" I sputtered the words out between sobs and heaves.

"Then you have to make me a promise." Mum extinguished her cigarette under the tap and washed the butt down the kitchen sink. "No more binge drinking, and if your grades haven't improved by the end of the year, the deal's off."

I had no choice in the matter. My life was here, in Melbourne, at Macleod College. God knows why I cared so much to stay enrolled in such a shithole.

I accepted the deal, and crossed my fingers behind my back.

I'd have to find a new vice.

Why do I feel physically ill doing this?

I haven't lived a life of shame, yet I am extremely ashamed to share it. All I want to do is stop writing. To delete every word. What am I hiding from? Is there a truth about me I am yet to discover? A truth I have kept protected somewhere behind the mirror?

I have accepted I spent a long time hating my mother for something she had no control over, I have accepted I was a reckless delinquent during high school. And I feel proud of the fact that I have ambition as an adult, and I have made a career for myself from point zero, so it's not as if there is nothing in my life to celebrate. In fact, there is probably more to celebrate than not, so what's my fucking problem?

You are my fucking problem.

If I dress you up the way I feel, I will not stop crying.

If I stop crying, I'll dress you up the way I should feel, but I will not stop feeling the way I shouldn't.

I am afraid that recording the poignant moments of the last thirty years will be the death of my carefully arranged sanity, my coping mechanism. I'm afraid it's going to set a new light under the need to run again, I'm afraid the mirror I see you in will break, and I'll have seven years bad luck.

I hate you. Do you hate me when I look at you? Have I been running from you all this time only to discover that you're a nobody, and actually not harmful? Are you really just me in the mirror? Why do you always look so different to how I remember myself?

And what if, somewhere inside you, is happiness?

Are you hiding it from me? You and your ridiculous parading around the house naked, showing off how one day your arse looks tight and toned, and on others like a big fat cow?

Okay, I get it. You're a transformer. You learnt that from me.

Can you show me how it works again? I've forgotten.

I'd like to be prepared for tomorrow.

By mid 1997, I had a new best friend. Her name was Kerry, a girl I'd known since my first year of high school, but connected with on a much deeper level during VCE (the last two years of high school in Victoria aimed towards gaining university entry) as we shared an interest in English, Literature, and Drama, three school subjects we took together and I was good at. If it wasn't for Kerry, I don't think I'd have gotten through the rest of high school. Because without really knowing it, our friendship guided me towards hanging out with a whole new group of students—the Artsy/Intellectual crowd who preferred learning and achieving over wagging and numbing the brain. Yes, I'd decided to 'pull my socks up.' And it saved me from being shipped off to Townsville. Unfortunately, though it seemed plausible for a while, it wasn't enough to tame my destructive reflection.

Kerry, being a theatre enthusiast and extremely articulate communicator, scored the job of directing the school play that year, *Twelfth Night* by William Shakespeare, and she cast me for the role of Olivia. On opening night in December of 1997, my fellow cast and I were teeming with adolescent adrenaline backstage.

"Guys, can you hear that?" Kerry said, gathering her long ginger hair into a bun which accentuated her pointy yet elegant nose and small rosy mouth.

"Hear what?" I said, simultaneously reciting my opening lines in my head.

"Shh." Kerry raised a finger to her lips. "Listen."

The mumbling voices and muffled footsteps of the congregating crowd triggered a thrill so deep it almost matched the high of drunkenness. Butterflies headbutted the lining of my stomach. I throve on the ambivalent fear.

Cash, a student two years younger than me (who looked and behaved two years older than me) playing Sebastian, winked in my direction. My skin tingled. For the first time ever, I had a real crush on someone. The kind of crush that smells like freedom and makes your heart flutter whenever you think about them. This was so different from anything I had ever experienced. For one, I wasn't drunk. And two, I didn't want to have sex with him, I wanted to *spend time* with this boy.

```
I do I know not what, and fear to find
Mine eye too great a flatterer for my mind.
Fate, show thy force: ourselves we do not owe;
What is decreed must be, and be this so.
```

When I left the stage after my first scene, Cash was standing behind the curtain.

"I'm going for a cig. Wanna come?" he said, winking again.

Outside, the scent of art class mixed with footie field grass and summer night air gave me goose bumps. I was nervous. I'd never been nervous in a situation like this. It was a sign that what I was feeling was real. And that realization made me even more nervous.

Cash smoked. I watched. When he tipped his head to the side as he dropped the cigarette butt on the ground, his thick black fringe fell in front of his crystal blue eyes. My stomach fluttered and I became conscious of my warm breath running through my nose and down my throat and into my lungs. He reached behind me and gently rested his hand on my lower back, then pulled me in close.

My entire body tensed up for a moment before I relaxed into his embrace. Our tongues slid inside each other's mouths. He tasted of mint and smoke. His kiss sent shivers through every limb.

The nerves evaporated from my skin as I realized I, a soon-to-be seventeen-year-old girl, was falling for a fifteen-year-old boy, and we would be targets for ridicule.

You'll never escape being different.

go

But I didn't care. Not really. I was used to it now. And in my eyes, Cash was a *man*.

"What about your girlfriend?" I said.

"I wanna be with you."

My mother wasn't there to watch me that night either. But I couldn't care less.

Because I'd found my new vice—the high of falling in love—and there was no room for a mother in a romantic relationship.

February 1998, my parents bought me tickets to see STOMP—a percussion performance group that was taking the world by storm—for my seventeenth birthday. Kerry and I had been looking forward to the concert for weeks. And as I was now working part-time in a store that sold things like candles and incense and dream catchers at Northland Shopping Centre, I felt like I was finally on my way into adulthood—into an era I could make my own decisions, choose who I wanted to spend time with, who not to spend time with, and very soon be able to move out of home—legitimately, and calmly, with an education.

All day during the lead-up to the concert, I listened to the one track I had on cassette over and over. Something about the persistent and raw percussion on trash cans and plastic containers, and whatever else they'd scavenged from the tip and turned into a drum, deeply resonated with me. For one, it further consolidated the fact that if there's a will there's a way (something my mother always used to say). If such brilliant music can be created with trash and raw talent, then brilliance, I figured, was purely derived from passion. And if this was the case, I could be brilliant too, no matter what resources I had at my disposal. Two, the beat of their 'drums' matched the beat of my heart. Sometimes deep, sometimes tinny. Sometimes soft, sometimes loud. Sometimes angry, sometimes proud. I could feel their rhythm as if it were my own private soundtrack. It spoke to me as clearly and deeply as if it had lyrics. *You are on your own*, they said. *But you are also your strongest and bravest ally. You don't need anyone if you have yourself.*

There was, however, an obstacle, as always, that threatened to stop me from going to this concert: Mum's health.

Come early evening, I sat on the edge of my bed, listening to her crying out in pain. It had become an everyday occurrence by now, as she was well and truly deep into a drug withdrawal—having now quit Valium for good—that would last for years. I wore psychological earplugs like a nun wore her habit. Mum was going through something I couldn't understand—she was often bed ridden and unable to move. Demetri rarely sat by her side to comfort her, and if he did, Mum had begged him to come. She had to beg me to come too. I rarely sat with her either. Especially that night. All I could think about was getting to the concert. Demetri was supposed to drive me to The Palais Theatre in St. Kilda where it was being held, and I wouldn't let anything or anyone stop me from going this time.

Mum moaned even louder and sobbed like a suffering animal. "I want to die."—a phrase uttered so often it soon lost all meaning to me. It had merely become another complaint, like one would complain about their sandwich not having enough mayo on it. None of us were yet aware that it was the drug withdrawal causing her so much pain. She kept going to the doctor for test after test after test for various fatal and debilitating diseases that never

go

came back with positive results.

I heard a siren. An ambulance pulled into our driveway.

I watched the flashing red lights flicker through my window and stared at my reflection in the glass.

I can't handle this anymore.
It's never going to stop, is it?
Then do something about it.
Like what?
We need to come first.

I could no longer blame my selfish thoughts on my reflection. We were one now. She'd trapped me on the wrong side of the glass.

I stepped out of my bedroom and tried to swallow the insults I wished to spit at my mother as she was being rolled out on a stretcher.

If you stop me from going, I'll never forgive you.
If you stop me from going, I'll ...

"Can I still go to the concert?" I asked. I internally cursed at myself for being so insensitive. Of course I cared. But I was also fed up with Mum's problems dictating my life. They weren't dictating my life. I was free to do what I pleased now that I'd got my shit together. But it *felt* like her problems were dictating my life because she was all I could think about, whether in a positive or negative light, she was there. In my head. Always in my head. Pounding, begging, pleading for attention, and at the same time, to not exist.

Stop existing. Kill yourself and we'd be better off.

Mum pulled the oxygen mask off her face, just before she was rolled outside, and said to Demetri between sobs, "Take her. It's okay. She should go. She deserves to go."

Relief flushed through me. I didn't even tell Kerry what had happened when I got there. As far as I was concerned, it was just another normal night at 80 Edwin Street.

A night I could be the Jessica in the glass.

How could I just push aside my mother's cries for help? I don't know. I look back on this day with such sorrow, wishing I could go back to show a little compassion for a woman enduring—and bravely, I might add—a scarring life experience that she would carry around with her for the rest of her life. Not only would she carry that pain and suffering forever, but she would carry around the guilt of 'not being the mother I deserved.' This was not her fault. She was thrust into a world that took hell and high water to live through, and escape from.

She did the best she could.

Cash and I quickly became serious, and I soon discovered that his mother had recently kicked a drug habit too. She had been addicted to speed, and due to that, Cash and his two brothers were separated. His two brothers lived with his father in New Zealand, and Cash had recently moved to Melbourne, Australia, to live with his mum, her partner, and baby half-sister.

No wonder we connected so fast, I thought. Both our mothers were victims of drug withdrawal. We had an unspoken bond. A vulnerability that only others with the same vulnerability could recognize.

"There are still times she craves it," Cash said one day during a lunch break when we were sitting on our own. "And she goes a bit mental."

I listened in silence, wondering whether or not to tell him about my mum.

"But Rich is really good. He helped her get clean, and he's really good at stopping her from doing it again. He's good for her."

I didn't know how to react. I'd spent so long making

go

myself numb to my mother's situation, that I'd lost all sense of compassion. How was I supposed to let go of everything I'd bottled up? How was I supposed to understand what Cash was feeling when I hadn't allowed myself to understand my own feelings?

So I faked it.

"Shit." I rubbed Cash on the back and gave him a comforting hug. "I'm sorry. That must be hard."

"Yeah. You know, it *is* hard." He picked at a loose thread on the knee of his school pants. "Watching her do so much unimportant shit around the house to try and take her mind off the cravings. Sometimes she gets really edgy, you know? And obsessive about stuff. Like she'll clean the oven over and over so she's doing something with her hands. And she takes it out on me and Rich sometimes, like, you know, yelling for no reason and shit. She apologizes though. And I just sorta ignore it and go to my room when she's like that. Not much else to do."

Cash looked into his lap. Was it a tear I noticed? Was he a guy that wasn't afraid of crying? Of showing his real emotions? This was so new to me.

I pressed my lips together and stroked Cash's cheek. I cared so much for this boy that I thought I should show it by getting teary. I did what my Drama teacher said: *think about something that makes you sad*. I thought about the ants. Those poor helpless ants whose world was so much bigger than mine, whose world was a war zone. They lived each and every day to collect food for the winter. Did they worry that a giant white Beetle would crush them on their journey? Did they live in constant fear and angst that their life was just a big fat dead end with a big fat darkness to look forward to?

I did.

Round and round I'd go, drawing curved lines through empty squares, hoping that one day, they'd be coloured in, hoping that one day, my actions would not simply be the same actions all over again—repeatedly striking through empty squares merely meeting their own tails.

"At least I've got Rich." Cash looked up briefly and smiled. "He's awesome. He warns me when Mum isn't in a good place. He protects me from it. I don't think Mum could do this without him either."

Rich protects him from it.
Rich protects him from it?

"Maybe you and my mum should meet," I said, without really considering the amount of explaining I'd have to do.

But as soon as I said that, a switch flicked.

I cried real tears and told Cash everything. About Mum's irrational rages, and how they made me hate her, and how we treated each other equally as bad. I'd never admitted that before, and it felt like a weight had been lifted off my shoulders. I also told him how I felt like I didn't have a 'Rich.' That Demetri retreated to a place of silence whenever Mum lost her temper. He never stood up for me. Or showed me what genuine care should look like—for me *or* my Mum. He never tried to reason with her if her behaviour seemed out of line. He never tried to reason with me when mine did either. He allowed Mum to drag me across the floor by my hair, for God's sake. And he allowed me to give Mum cold heartless looks when she was pleading for my help. As far as I was concerned, I didn't really have a father, I had a brother who was trying to escape the burden of my mother as much as I was.

Did I *blame* him for that? Probably. Is it why I don't

go

want to have children? Do I feel like I would essentially be a single mother despite Serafeim being a faithful and reliable partner for the last ten years?

I finished telling Cash how I'd thought about killing myself. I blamed it, out loud, on not being able to deal with my mum's behaviour. But when I uttered those words, it felt like a mammoth lie. Mum's behaviour was *not* the reason I wanted to kill myself. Yes, it may have heightened it, but it wasn't the *reason*. I didn't *know* they real reason why. Was I mad? Or was I just overreacting to this overpowering sense of sadness that attacked me in rock-infested oil-ridden waves when I least expected it? Though I couldn't identify it as depression at the time, I would eventually learn that that's what it was. I would discover that there is no reason for those feelings. And I would have to live with them, and learn how to use them, just like my arms and legs.

When the bell rang for class, Cash and I agreed, that yes, our mothers should meet.

Eventually they did meet, and formed a great relationship too. Whenever Cash's mother would come to pick him up from our house, she'd end up staying and having a chat. One time I eavesdropped on them as they were talking about their drug-withdrawal coping mechanisms. Another time Cash's mum came over to our house in the middle of the night when Demetri had contracted a staph infection from the hospital after having a hernia removed. She was armed with powdered vitamin C and a life's worth of medical advice. I think it's safe to say she saved him from a more serious secondary-infection that night.

While I was with Cash, things calmed down in my head—a lot. My mother's withdrawal symptoms persisted, but I did a great job of blocking them out without so much coldness, and she did a great job of hiding them from me, as I focussed all my energy on my studies so I would 'be the first person in our family to attend university.' Mum had expressed how much she wanted that for me, and I also wanted it for myself. Despite my desire to pursue a career in music, I knew now that without an education to fall back on, I would be stuck living a life behind a cash register, and the idea sickened me. That pharmacy left scars.

I didn't *completely* stop getting pissed at parties, but I became a little bit more responsible with my drinking habits, and I stopped trying to numb myself every weekend. I don't know if it was being in love with Cash, or my thriving friendship with Kerry, who was an excellent influence on me, but the voice of my reflection quietened down for a while. She was there, but more focussed on pushing me in the right scholarly direction rather than trying to repel my mother. (Or she was pushing me in the right scholarly direction so that I *could* repel my mother.)

My need to run subsided ever so slightly, or at least my relationship with Cash enabled me to ignore it, because there was nowhere I wanted to run to except whatever location Cash was at.

Every lunch and recess, Cash and I would hang out in the same place, with Kerry and the other cast members of *Twelfth Night*. Being a part of that production created such a strong bond between us, that we became long-term faithful friends despite being a mix of age groups. Many of us are still in touch today, and whenever I go back to Australia for a visit, and we find an opportunity to catch up face-to-face, it's like no time at all has come between us. Cash was the youngest, Gary, Vik, and Jonas, the

go

next year up, and Kerry and I the eldest. Clearly, right there, is something else Kerry and I had in common—we got along better with boys than girls.

Cash and I would often sit on a school yard bench before classes began for the day, huddled in each other's embrace, stealing short kisses when we thought no-one was looking, planning where we would be and at what time so that we could steal more hugs and kisses during brief school corridor passings. We'd take advantage of every second at the train station on our way home from school, both of us pining for the weekend when we could both sleep in the same bed at the house of whomever in our group was holding a get-together. Yes, a 'get-together.' This group of friends didn't have let's-get-shit-faced parties, they held civilized get-togethers. This didn't mean we wouldn't drink or smoke. But we wouldn't obliterate our brains doing so. And we talked. Real adult conversations. And this allowed us to bond on a level I'd not yet experienced in my lifetime.

For once in my adolescent life, I was happy.

And for that, I have my mother to thank.

One early evening at Jonas's house, the six of us sat in his backyard, slowly swigging from bottles of Strongbow (legally bought for us by his parents). Kerry sat on Vik's skinny lap, stroked her fingers through his silky brown curls, and kissed his Jewish-looking nose. This affection was not sexual in the slightest. These boys were like brothers to us, and we all often exchanged hugs and kisses like we were family. (Though I'm sure the boys had to tame an erection from time to time, as Kerry and I were not only good-looking young women, but completely uninhibited around our friends.)

I sat in Cash's lap and leaned my cheek on top of his head.

"I wish we could all be in another play this year," Jonas said, jiggling his knees up and down and scratching the blonde 'fluff' on his chin.

"That would be so cool," Cash said, wrapping his arms around me.

"Yeah," everyone hummed and nodded in agreement.

"Well," Kerry said, sliding off Vik's lap and clapping her hands in the air. "I'm going to direct *Cosi* for my Theatre Studies folio task. Auditions start next week. You'll all come, right?"

"Shit yeah!" Jonas said, grinning so wide I could almost see his molars.

"Sick," Gary said, nodding with a subtle grin on his face and then taking a swig from his bottle. He was the chubby quiet one in our group, but he laughed like an ambulance siren, and played air guitar whenever The Mighty Mighty Bosstones or Rancid were on the stereo.

I took the last sip of my Strongbow and went into Jonas's kitchen to grab myself another from the fridge, daydreaming about the potential excitement of being in another play together. As I closed the fridge door, Cash approached me from behind, slid his arms around my waist, and rested his chin on my shoulder. I brushed my cheek against his as I turned to face him, the scent of his soapy fresh cologne pulling me in closer. Cash leant in for a kiss and brushed his tongue and lower lip against my top one. He took the bottle out of my hand, rested it on the counter, and weaved his fingers through mine.

Cash looked into my eyes and smiled. "I love you, Jess."

Without a moment of hesitation, I said, "I love you too," and kissed him.

It was the first time we'd uttered those words, but it

go

felt so natural—like we had declared these feelings from the very beginning. There was nothing unfamiliar or doubtful about it. We really were legitimate high school sweethearts.

But due to Cash being so young, we never had sex. Despite a couple of attempts, it didn't happen. I think he was afraid, or nervous, or both. So I didn't push, and I was okay with that.

I think it further consolidated the idea that you didn't need sex to be in love, or love to have sex. They had become two very separate things to me now. Sex equalled exhibitionistic rebelliousness. Love equalled platonic affection.

The next week at school, Cash auditioned for the role of Doug, a pyromaniac who loved sexual innuendo (interestingly!), and I auditioned for the role of Julie, who was dependent on drugs (double-interestingly!). Cash got the role, but I didn't. Kerry said another student fit the role better. And though I was disappointed, I admired Kerry for not feeling the need to cast me simply because I was her friend. She did what was best for the play and her folio task. Kerry had already bloomed into a beautiful young woman and she was confident in herself and in the choices she made. Kerry inspired me with her passion and determination to succeed in something she loved.

Which made me realize ... it was time I followed *my* heart and got serious about my music.

Katherine, the violinist of my on and off again duet, and I decided to get real in mid 1998. We recruited a drummer named Joe, and a cellist named Lin, and we became a band. We started off being called *String Bridge*, and then soon became *spAnk*.[11]

---
11 That cap's not a typo. You'll notice also that I ended up titling my debut novel with the first name of the band.

Every week we'd rehearse at each other's houses in pursuit of a clear goal: when we finished high school, we'd start looking into playing gigs around Melbourne.

One of our Music teachers, Mr Hart, soon suggested we enter the Australian National Battle of the Bands competition, in which every school in the country selected a band to represent them. In order to enter we had to record a video performing one of our original songs. So we did.

Katherine's mother hung a big white sheet across a wall in their living room. We sat in front of it with our instruments and mimed to the track Mr Hart helped us record with school facilities.[12] Katherine's elder sister filmed and edited it for us. (Unfortunately, I have no idea where this video is now.) It wasn't the greatest of videos, but it was the best we could do with what we had. Mr Hart submitted our video, and told us that he'd let us know the results when he knew.

We waited months.

Until one day when I had my head down in an Australian History class, Mr Hart rapped on the door. Everyone looked up as he inched it open and apologized for the interruption.

"Can I borrow Miss Bell for a minute?" With a cheeky grin on his face, he strung all the words together as one.

"You *may* borrow Jessica for a minute, Mr Hart," Mr Thompson, my history teacher, said in jest, making everyone in class chuckle—probably more at the dorky expression on his face than the modal verb correction.

"Watch it, Tommie," Mr Hart said, touching his nose. "Not in front of the kids. You might influence them." Mr Hart and Mr Thompson laughed. I internally blushed at the kick I got out of such a geeky conversation.

---

[12] The song is 'Little Body Bleeds,' and you can listen to the recording on my Bandcamp page, here: *bit.ly/spAnk*

go

I collected my books, as the home-time bell was going to ring any minute, and stepped into the corridor.

"You'll never believe it, Jess, but you did it."

"What do you mean?" I wouldn't believe it until he spelt it out.

"You and five other bands from Victoria are in the State Finals. You're going to perform at Festival Hall.[13] It seats five thousand people."

My breath caught in my throat. "Oh my God!"

"Go on, go tell the others," he said. "I'll fill you in properly tomorrow."

The bell rang and I bolted down the corridor towards the Year 12 lockers, weaving through swarms of students gushing out of classrooms, my heart beating like it was on steroids.

"We're in, we're in! We did it!" I called out from a distance when I caught sight of Katherine and Joe collecting their bags.[14]

Katherine flicked her head in my direction and her jaw dropped. "What?"

"We're in the State Finals," I cried, at the top of my lungs.

Katherine and I squealed and jumped around like Beatles fans. Even Joe, who at first grinned casually like a little boy, trying not to giggle, let loose pretty quickly and started punching and kicking the air and yelling, "Yes yes yes!"

This was a victory for us.

I'm going to be a rock star.

You are, in fact, going to rule the world.

---

13 I'm not certain it was Festival Hall, but it's the only concert hall in Melbourne which seems to visually match what I remember.
14 The cellist was from another school.

We stepped onto the massive stage at Festival Hall for the State Finals of the Battle of the Bands in October of 1998. Katherine and Lin looked around in silent panic. They couldn't find where they were supposed to plug their instruments in. And neither could I. My breathing slowed down. The murmur of the crowd, my own panicked thoughts, and the yabber of backstage crew blended together as if we were under water. These men in black pranced around us, half hunched over, trying to be inconspicuous I imagine, poking the ends of power leads at us and pointing silently to little boxes located randomly on the ground. I had no idea what was what, but sure enough, when I stuck a lead into the pick-up clamped to my twelve-string, and then into the box indicated to me, the feedback was deafening.

I quickly faced my guitar in the opposite direction, praying that the feedback would stop. It did. But it kept threatening to erupt with little squeaks as I navigated my way to the stool in front of the microphone.

My first ever performance in front of a real audience, and not only was the tech playing devil's advocate, but it was in front of thousands.

Lin must have seen the terror on my face. She touched my upper arm and smiled, her head cocked to the side. "It's okay, Jess. It will be okay. We've got this."

I took a deep breath and nodded. A guy behind the curtain flashed two fingers at me. We had two minutes before we had to start. I let everyone know and the four of us took our positions. My guitar was still squeaking, but I quickly whipped out my tuner and made sure each string was in tune.

The lights dimmed.

Joe counted us in, "One, two, three, and—"

go

I started too early, but being the talented instrumentalists that my band members were, they smoothly adjusted to it and we continued in time.

But I couldn't hear Joe's congas. *No-one* could hear the congas. And the hot lights were slowly but surely expanding the strings on my guitar and detuning them.

We stole quick glances at each other. We understood. Luckily Joe was sitting to the side of us, rather than behind us, so we were able to watch his movement to stay in time. Unfortunately, keeping an eye on Joe's movements didn't change the off notes that swam to the forefront of every strum.

There were a few more hiccups—like me forgetting the lyrics and singing gobbledegook—but we recovered. The song wasn't performed at its best, but we made it through.

The applause was slack. I knew then that the audience had probably heard the exact same conglomeration of anti-dynamic noise that we had heard.

I stepped off stage shaking. The buzz I'd felt before the performance had been squashed like the helpless ants I'd tried to save in my driveway as a child. Above all, I was disappointed that the tech caused us to screw up. We were so much better than what we'd had the opportunity to show.

"Joe, no more congas," I said. "Let's put you on a real drum kit. I'm going to buy an electric guitar. And let's look into getting professional pick-ups for the strings. The ones from school suck." I wasn't going to let that pathetic excuse of a show happen to us again.

We all gave each other a high five, and then had a group hug.

Mr Hart gave us a pat on our backs when he greeted us

outside. All he had was praise to give. But I know he was just trying to be encouraging.

We didn't make the Nationals.

But we were just getting warmed up.

It neared the end of 1998 and I was soon to sit my final exams. I'd submitted my university preferences: 1. Melbourne Uni, Bachelor of Arts, Creative Writing Major (Score of 96.8 needed), 2. Deakin Uni, Bachelor of Arts, Professional Writing Major (Score of 89.6 needed), 3. La Trobe Uni, Bachelor of Arts, Archaeology Major (Score of 56.5 needed). I desperately wanted the slot at Deakin, but I put Melbourne first because of its prestige, and I knew there was no way I was going to get a score of 96.8 out of 100. 89.6 however? Entirely possible. I was confident I would get a score in the 80s, so I had my fingers crossed I'd just slip in. If not, the idea of Archaeology fascinated me, having spent plenty of time in Greece. La Trobe only had an English major, and I wasn't so keen on analysing other people's books—I wanted to learn how to write my own, so Archaeology seemed the next best thing to select. And if I didn't like it, I could switch to an English Major in second semester without losing the credits.

I put my head down and studied. Hard.

Through migraine after migraine, and practice essay after practice essay, I got through one of the toughest periods of my high school life. It passed by in a whirlwind and I hardly remember a moment of it except that my mother, regardless of the pain she was in, put on a brave face and tried to be as encouraging as possible. She made me food, coffee, tried to be quiet when I slept, listened when I'd complain, and praised my ability to tough it out. And even though we hadn't discussed our feelings about

go

the previous few years, I felt like we might be on our way to mending the hurt.

On some occasions, though, I would talk about school, and she'd smile and nod, and make 'hmm' noises of agreement, but wouldn't actually hear a thing. Sometimes I would repeat the same sentence multiple times, to test it out, and she would react as if the information was completely new. Most times I could tell when my words would dissolve into thin air. Mum's eyes would glaze over, and she'd suck really hard on her cigarettes. All I had to do was look into her eyes, see the glaze, the stiffness in her smile, and I'd know she was having a 'bad day.'

It drove me nuts. But I left her alone.

There *were* times in 1998, however, when she seemed 'normal.' On those days I was able to invite friends over, and she'd actually spend time with us as if a part of the gang.

One Friday after school, I called to see if Mum was doing okay, and asked whether I could bring home company. She said yes, and Kerry, Cash, Jonas, Vik, and Gary came over to my house. I can't remember what we had for dinner, but I imagine it would have been something easy like pasta or pizza.

After we ate, Mum sat all the boys on one side of the living room, and Kerry and I on the other side.

"So, I'm curious," Mum said to the guys, as she parked her butt in her chair and lit a cigarette with a smirk. "What is it that boys your age think about?"

I squinted at Mum, wondering where she was going with this. I knew she liked to tease everyone about their love lives, and to have confronting conversations with my friends, but sometimes I couldn't gauge how far she'd go. I think, however, that I was the only one embarrassed by it. My friends adored my mother. She was the 'coolest mum ever.'

Cash sat on the end of the couch, closest to my Mum, with an expression of pride and belonging on his face. He had very much become a part of the family now, and Mum and Demetri had accepted him as one of their own. Jonas sat with his hands folded in his lap, next to Cash, Vik next to Jonas in a similar position, and Gary on the other end with one leg hung over the armrest, playing with the spiky dog collar around his neck.

Cash casually took a cigarette from Mum's packet of Peter Jackson Extra Milds on the coffee table. Mum passed him her lighter. They exchanged knowing glances. Jonas said, "Ya know, boy stuff," and laughed. Vik piped up and added, "We can't say the stuff we think in front of Jess 'n' Kerry!"

Mum laughed. "Well, you must masturbate a lot." There's no way she was going to let them off that easily.

I groaned and Kerry gasped like someone suddenly shoved a stick up her bum. Then Kerry and I pissed ourselves laughing, which was contagious, and the boys joined in too, until Jonas, always the one to put his best foot forward, said, "Yeah. I reckon I try to feed the chooks about ten times a day." Vik nodded in agreement. Gary scoffed and said, "Yeah, me too."

Mum looked at Cash with her eyebrows raised. I didn't know whether I should jump in and save him from embarrassment or not. Kerry whispered in my ear, "Your mum's hilarious," as Cash said, "Pass" and chuckled in embarrassment, looking over at me. I laughed.

If only you all knew the half of it.

"Shit. I'm gonna crack a fat." Vik stood up, covered the front of his pants with his hand, and stormed out of the

go

room. I laughed so hard my stomach ached, and my ears felt like they were going to pop. Then Vik walked back into the living room wearing one of my dresses with a red bra over the top of it, and we pissed ourselves laughing some more.

"It suits you, Vik," Kerry said with a wink. "Don't you think, Erika?"

Mum nodded and laughed, and everyone else agreed.

I could have lived a hundred doses of that evening. My mum was alive. Really alive. And I hoped and prayed she wouldn't wake up the next morning with another wave of debilitating withdrawal. I wanted everyone to be like this all the time. I wanted *her* to be like this all the time: happy.

And then it hit me.

All this was going to end in a couple of months when high school finished. Kerry and I would be off to university, and the boys would still be in school. All this happiness was going to be over. Cash and I would be apart a lot. Our lives would be completely different.

This light I was living at the end of a very long and truncated tunnel was ... about to go dark again.

So instead of playing it out, giving this new life a chance to begin and adjust to my current circumstances, the voice of my reflection came back. And for some fucked up reason, I thought it would be a good idea to destroy something that wasn't broken.

I arrived at Cash's house in a street lined with flourishing plane trees. His mum greeted me with the warmth and love she had always offered and told me to sit at the counter while she finished the dishes.

Cash wasn't home from school yet, so I sat at the kitchen counter and told his mum the reason I was visiting as she washed. She didn't seem in the slightest bit shocked at what I told her and assured me she understood. But she paused a moment, looked out of the kitchen window, and sighed as she hung her head to the side.

"He's going to be devastated," she said. "I'm glad you told me first."

I nodded, understanding she was relieved to be at home to offer Cash support when I left.

The front door opened, and there stood Cash. "Jess!" He dropped his school bag on the floor and held out his arms. "What are you doing here?" Our visits were usually planned, so it must have seemed odd. The huge smile plastered on his face disappeared as soon as I turned to face him and burst into tears.

"What's wrong?" he said. I looked at his mother.

"Take him to the back room," she said with a flick of her head, as if I was about to interrogate and torture him like a terrorist.

I nodded and slid off the bar stool.

"What's going on?" Cash flicked a quick glance at his mum, who was now drying her hands on a tea towel and looking at the floor.

I led Cash to the back room and we sat on the edge of his parents' bed. He gently took my hand and held it in his lap. He must have thought something bad had happened to me or my mum—his eyes grew teary and his brow puckered.

Tears poured from my eyes in a waterfall of regret. I didn't know what I was doing. I didn't want to be there, causing so much pain to myself or to Cash or to his parents who had grown to love me like their own. I didn't want to do this at all, but *my reflection* ... she said it was for the best.

go

And I'd started it now. I had to follow through.

"I think we should break up," I said. "I—"

—didn't have time to say another word because Cash's fist went through the wall.

I stood up in shock and tried to stop him from hurting himself, but he wouldn't let me touch him.

"Get out," he said.

"Cash, I'm—"

"Get out, I said!"

I swung open the door and ran down the corridor back to the kitchen. Rich had just arrived and it seemed Cash's mum had filled him in on the details.

I stood there, in the doorway, bawling my eyes out. Cash's parents remained behind the kitchen counter with their arms crossed. The looks on their faces did not match their body language at all. They were sad for me, and not at all angry. I think they may have felt guilty about feeling sorry for me as well as Cash.

"Cash has put a hole in your wall," I stammered through gasping heaves.

His mother nodded, and leaned forward, resting her hands on the edge of the counter.

"Good luck, Jessica." She hung her head.

I picked up my bag, and walked out.

I never saw them again.

I lay in the darkness, with my headphones on. In my Discman I had Elliott Smith's *Either/Or* album on repeat. I listened to it three times straight through, until the early hours of the morning. Sobbing, sobbing, sobbing, hitting my head, cursing myself, cursing my existence, then consoling myself, telling myself I had done the right thing, that I needed to be free, I needed to move on, far from high school, far from what that place represented, far from everyone who took me back. I wanted to live a life I didn't need to run from, and that meant a life without memories. Then I'd sob and sob and sob some more, berating myself some more, until I was so exhausted I fell asleep, woke up with a migraine, and cried again when I realized the horrible thing I had just done.

My grief lasted way too long for a person who'd done the breaking up.

The next morning I wouldn't get out of bed. Mum gave me my space until around midday, when she came in with a cup of hot Nescafé and Milo mix with lots of milk, and opened my blinds.

She sat on the edge of the bed and stroked my head.

"Come on, Juice. Sit up. Drink some of this." She sniffed. She'd been crying, her nose shiny and red, her glasses a touch foggy.

I inched myself up with my elbows and Mum propped the cushions behind my back.

I started to cry before I could take my first sip. Mum did too, and squeezed the top of my right thigh.

"I don't understand, Juice," she said, wiping away her tears with an overused tissue she pulled from her sleeve. "Why did you do this?" Mum's voice was calm—a half-whisper.

I shrugged, and said through intermittent sobs, "I don't know. I felt like I needed to. I don't know."

Mum pressed her lips together and looked into her lap.

"Well, Demetri and I are here for you. It's heartbreaking, but we trust you made the right decision for *you*. I'm sure you know deep down why you did it. We just want you to be happy. If you're happy, we're happy."

I nodded and took a sip of my beverage. The milky

mocha taste warmed my chest and momentarily soothed my aching mind.

Mum took the mug from me and put it on the floor by the bed, then she took my hands and squeezed them. Hers were cold and clammy—a constant—but her eyes shone with concern, and the warmth of her love trickled through.

"Cash aside ... *are* you happy?"

What is happiness?

So far there was nothing in my life that relieved me of the fish hooks floating around in my chest, the rotting pendulum hitting my temples over and over, or the voice of my reflection which seemed to be on a mission to make me feel and think the contrary to everything and anything.

Writing music wasn't my saviour.

Writing music made me feel even worse because it summoned melancholia like a snake whisperer.

The world I lived in had become a more elaborate version of our driveway, and I was an ant. It would only be a matter of time before everything I had worked and strived for would be squashed and buried in the earth along with my flesh and bones. And if nothing lasted forever, what was the point in beginning?

I looked Mum in the eye. "Yes. I'm happy."

Mum gave me a big long hug, and encouraged me to get up and have something to eat. When she left the room, I sat up in bed and looked at the photo of Laurel, my friend who'd died in Year 8, which still sat on my bookshelf.

Thinking about her death sent me mixed messages:

Life is too short and it can end at any moment. You need to make the most of it.

You can die at any time without warning, so what's the point of even trying to be good at anything?

Oh, the bliss of being dead and not having to worry about anything anymore. Suicide is still a possibility. What are you afraid of?

Live carelessly and recklessly, and stop worrying. If you're going to die, you're going to die. You might as well have fun getting there.

I grabbed my head and fell face first into my pillow. I bit down hard onto the feather-filled fabric, curled the sides of the pillow around my head, and screamed as loud and as long as my breath allowed.

My lips and face and eyes and throat burned.

I needed to run. Fast.

But from what?

There was no longer anything I needed to run from ... except myself.

part four
1999-2005

part four
1999-2005

Why do you make me feel like I'm drowning in my own blood? I always want to run from you. Jump on a random plane, change my name, live a new life. But you will always follow.

I know, in reality, that this is irrational, so I'll search for a 'cure' that is a little more sane. You tell me I'll screw up. That I should leave Serafeim, but of course, it has to be when he's at his bar one night so he can't see what's going on, and of course, I should never tell him where I'm going—just leave and let him think I am dead.

That would be heartless, because deep down I am a heartless person. You tell me so every time I look at you. You scold me, belittle me, and I admit that I'd be better off accepting my life as it is so that I don't hurt anyone, even you.

I'll just obsess over work again, tick things off a list that I purposely keep adding to so I'm never finished, so I never have to sit and look at myself—the self I see without the mirror. I'll mute my tears until my head hurts, and finally retreat, once more, behind my wall of emotional disconnection.

Please don't be alarmed if I don't come to see you for a while.

You're ugly this month.

You are a bad influence on my heart.

With an entry score of 82.6 (which I was extremely proud of considering my rapid shift in attitude) I missed out on getting into Deakin's BA in Professional Writing. So in 1999, I enrolled into a Bachelor of Arts with a major in Archaeology at La Trobe University, Bundoora. Kerry, being the genius that she is, got an entry score of 99.6, and was accepted into Melbourne University. However, after being disgusted by the elitist attitudes of the tutors and fellow students during orientation, she decided she didn't want to swim in such circles, turned the offer down, and attended La Trobe as well. That was a blessing for me because it meant we were able to hold each other's hands during this exciting, but challenging, transition in our lives.

Now being a driver's licence holder and the owner of a crème Holden Gemini station wagon which fit a band's worth of music equipment, I was able to get from A to B with ease. I'd spend many an afternoon and evening hanging out at Kerry's house after lectures, chatting about her plans to run an amateur theatre company and my plans to have *spAnk* playing gigs around Melbourne. I had also started saving to record a professional demo with money earned from an on-campus job in a Chinese takeaway store.

Katherine, Lin, Joe, and I continued to rehearse every opportunity we got. We did record that demo, and Mum, with her brand new Nikon camera (Hard Candy had now ceased and she had taken up photography to keep herself occupied) took some band photos of us[15], put together a press pack, and gave us her industry contacts to send copies of the demo out. Not only did this lead to us being played on local and national radio a number of times, but we also performed on Channel 31, an independent TV station. It wasn't long before we were performing regular gigs in pubs around Melbourne, such as The Evelyn Hotel and The Punters Club (which is now a pizza bar called Bimbo Deluxe) on Brunswick Street in Fitzroy. We even

---

15 I have tried and tried to locate these but to no avail. If you have any old copies of *Inpress* and *Beat Magazine* from 1999 and 2000 you may find us there.

played at a venue called Revolver Upstairs in Chapel Street, Prahran, as one of the supporting acts for Killing Heidi, an Australian rock band who were nominated in seven categories and won four trophies at the ARIA Music Awards of 2000. *spAnk* was now a real thing, and the prospect of becoming well-known kept us eagerly striving for more and more.

In the meantime, I kept my depression at bay by experimenting with my look (and inadvertently my personality) so often that students at Uni sometimes failed to recognize me. A few of my different looks were: 1) green, orange, and white extensions in my hair, dressed all in body-fitted black, so that I looked like a punk version of Olivia Newton John in Grease. 2) The casual/cool jeans and suit jacket combo that made me feel like an intellectual, but artsy at the same time, and a little Julia Roberts from the final scene of *Pretty Woman*. 3) Bright red hair with a bright red ponytail wig and tight, revealing and sometimes glittery disco-esque clothing which had a passerby once run up to me asking if I was Nicole Kidman. 4) Jet black hair with elaborate black eye-liner and a mix between 90s rock chick and 80s Material Girl look. That one had people calling me Cleopatra.

After one semester of Archaeology, I realized it wasn't for me. Though I made up excuses along the lines of disinterest, it was the fact that I was hopeless at mathematics, and this inhibited my ability to pass the Research Methods module, which counted for 50% of my overall score. I couldn't trust myself to put my head down and improve my mathematics skills, so I switched to an English major.

Though it was mostly focussed on literature analysis, there were a few subjects available to me that strengthened my creative writing skills: Fiction Writing, Nonfiction

Writing, and Screenwriting. Of course, I chose to take all three. They were the only three subjects I excelled in with ease. The rest I had to work as hard as I had done in Archaeology, which was disappointing, but I managed. My mother always joked that I was lazy. But it wasn't that at all. If I didn't enjoy doing something, I didn't see any reason to put more effort in than what was necessary.

For the first year or so of university, I wouldn't say I was 'happy,' but I was psychologically steady. Not numb, just redirected. I had to be. Everything was so new that all my energy went into navigating the possibilities of this new world I lived in. I looked into joining political clubs despite not understanding a thing about politics. I looked into joining charity organizations, environmental campaigns, hosting a show on the La Trobe radio station, writing for the university newspaper, becoming a part of the backstage crew for forthcoming theatre productions. Anything that was different to what my heart usually gravitated towards.

I wanted to taste it all. But I didn't end up trying any of it, because …

… my mind was stronger than my heart and my mind gravitated towards alcohol.

I started binge drinking again when I cottoned on to La Trobe's Bar Night at The Eagle which was held every Thursday from 5 p.m. and sold very cheap drinks. Almost every Thursday night I joined hundreds of sexually charged and overexcited eighteen-year-olds with the newfound freedom of being at a legal age to purchase alcohol.

And I. Went. Nuts.

No more mother to tell you what to do.

go

You're an adult now.

You earn your own money. You pay board.

You have a car.

You could move out of home if you wanted to.

You're free.

Your life is one hundred per cent yours. Make it yours.

I'd drink and vomit and pass out in public every week. My friends would carry me to their cars, houses, to taxis, to trains or buses. I had sex with friends, and friends of friends, and didn't think twice about it. I even engaged in a threesome with a guy and girl I knew who were a couple very much in love. I often wonder whether I was the reason they broke up. The guilt still eats at me when I think about it.

But my body was now conditioned to not only *cope* with this abuse, but bounce back from it within hours. Which meant it didn't stop me from functioning day to day. It didn't stop me from achieving acceptable grades. It didn't stop me from getting *spAnk* on stage, or radio, or TV. I was getting everything I wanted, and thought I needed. So why question whether my behaviour was good for me or not? I had essentially become a functioning alcoholic.

It would take a couple more years of spiralling further out of control for me to find out.

Because Katherine attended Melbourne Uni, and we only needed one band member to be enrolled in order to be eligible, *spAnk* entered the Melbourne University Band Competition in September of 1999, the first round of the Australian National Campus Band Competition. The winner would go on to compete at the State Finals, and the State Finalists at the Nationals, representing their university.

We competed in the first round at The Evelyn Hotel in Brunswick Street, and we performed the best gig I can remember. No tech glitches, faulty notes, or forgotten lyrics tainted us that day. The gods were on our side. And we won. I still have the Maton Mastersound MS500 Sunburst electric guitar that was awarded to us that day.[16]

When our performance was over, the bass player from one of the competing bands—a lanky heavy metal guy with long mousy brown hair and blue eyes who had been shouting praise from the audience—approached me and slurred something along the lines of, "A chick on guitar is *hot*. A chick with a dick, man."

I laughed. Or maybe I ignored him. I can't really remember because it took me by surprise. It was the first time someone had tried to pick me up in an 'adult' situation. I wasn't stumbling into his arms as a hopeless teenage drunk stripped of inhibition. This was the real world. And since witnessing everything my mother had gone through, and I had vowed to never drink before a performance because of it, I was completely sober. (Keeping the alcohol off the table at gigs, in my mind, meant I was being a responsible adult.)

Two seconds later the guy was dragged away by one of his band members, and then I heard a bang on the pub-front window. I turned around, and the guy had flattened his hands and face against the glass, waxing lyrical into misty condensation. I smirked, and turned away to watch the band that was currently on stage, the flutter of flattery multiplying in my stomach.

The seed for craving attention was securely planted.

I went to the toilets and looked at myself in the mirror.

---

16 I actually ended up exchanging it for a bright red and white version.

Random strands of my bright red shoulder-length hair were messily fastened to my scalp with bobby pins. *Who are you?* My black eyeliner had slightly melted into the flecks of silver glitter on my eyelids from the hot stage lights. *Do you really know?* My cheeks were flushed and my lips dry. I needed a beer, but I decided I wouldn't have one. *Are you happy?* I looked left and right and under the gaps of toilet cubicle doors to see if I was alone. I was. *Are you sad?* I pouted and turned my head side to side, adjusted my breasts in my bra. *Are you angry?* Pulled my red nylon stretch mesh shirt tautly over my flesh. *Are you mad?* Applied red lipstick and kissed the mirror. *Do you ... care?* I noticed for the first time, that I had become a woman. *You are talented, beautiful, they love you—use it.* A woman, who I believed, would one day become a famous rock star. And from that point forward, achieving fame as a rock star was all I could think about, and I was ready to do anything to get it.

I didn't do anything to get it. I went with the natural flow of a slow-building career. But it was motivating to think about my future with a bit of drama added to the mix. After all, drama was what I was used to.

Regardless, this newfound determination drove me upwards and onwards. Once again, I took it easy on booze, gained control of my wants and desires, grasped— even though ever so slightly—the importance of looking after myself. If I was going to make it in this industry it wouldn't do me any good to become a drug-fucked victim of suicide by the age of twenty-seven.

I thought back to the tenderness Cash and I shared. I missed him—the gentle quiet moments when we'd sit together in the school yard, hand in hand, my head resting on his shoulder. When the world became insignificant—a mere surface to tread on.

That was happiness.
You need another Cash.
It is the only thing that's going to save you.

Unfortunately, *spAnk* didn't play with the same precision at the State Finals a month later and we didn't make it to the Nationals. But it didn't discourage us. We continued to grow, and consistently pick up gigs in pubs around Melbourne.

After finishing our performance at the State Finals, I hung around in the crowd to watch the other acts. The tall lanky metal head with mousy brown hair inched through the crowd and held out his hand.

"Hi, I'm Craig," he said. I instantly recognized him and blushed. "Your band is awesome."

"Thanks." I smiled and shook his hand. I neglected to tell him my name.

"I'm sorry about my drunken slurring at The Evelyn," he yelled over the noise of the music and crowd. "That was, uh, embarrassing."

I laughed and said, "No worries."

"Actually—" Craig bent over slightly and spoke into my ear so he didn't have to yell. "I've been waiting for this night to come so I could see you again."

"What?" I said, stretching out the word in disbelief. "You liked our music that much?"

Craig smiled, looked at the stage, and took a swig from his bottle of Carlton Draught. "Yeah, but ..." he hesitated. "That's not what I meant."

I puckered my brow and cocked my head to the side. Craig laughed nervously and turned to face me.

"I meant ... I came to see *you*." Craig pointed the nozzle of his beer bottle at my chest.

"Oh," I said. "Interesting."

Interesting? That's all you can find to say to this good looking and charming guy who clearly you have a lot in common with, I mean, hello? He's a bassist in a metal band?

I cleared my throat and tried again. "Uh ... thank you?" I snorted. I never snorted.

What has got into you?

Craig nodded and looked towards the stage again, taking another swig of his beer. I swallowed and took a deep breath. Craig was cute. And he seemed like a gentle guy, despite the violent aggression he showed on stage.

"Um ... so have you been playing in Junkdust[17] long?" I said, in an attempt to keep him there.

His eyes lit up and he launched into a five-minute history of how they came to be. To cut a long story short, and as far as I can remember, his younger brother, who was a student at Melbourne Uni, was jamming with the singer/guitarist as a hobby. And when they found out about the competition, they decided to become a band and compete. They were able to find a drummer, but they were still missing a bassist. Craig wasn't even a bassist, he was a guitarist. But his brother convinced him to play the bass for the band so that they could enter. They put together their set in less than a month.

My question seemed to break the ice, and we talked about our bands and music until I had to drive Joe and his drum kit home. In that time I found out Craig was a fellow Pisces and five years older than me. I also found out that his sister's birthday was the same as my mother's. Which freaked me out because Cash's mother's

---

17 The name of the band is fictional to protect the privacy of the man I've named Craig.

birthday was the same as my mother's, and his brother's the same as mine.[18]

Craig also had a love of fixing up old Valiant cars, and drove around in a big dirty white Chrysler VJ Valiant Charger.

I gave him my phone number.

I wrote it on the back of his event pass and signed it, *Chick with a dick*.

Craig hadn't realized he didn't know my name until he called the house the following week and didn't know who to ask for when my mother picked up. Mum came into my bedroom saying that there was a strange guy on the phone asking for the singer of *spAnk*.

I took the phone and held it to my ear.

"Hello?"

"Um, hey, it's um Craig. How are ya?"

"I'm great. How are you?" My heart picked up pace and my cheeks grew warm.

"I'm not sure. I don't think your mum was very impressed I didn't know your name. I couldn't exactly ask for *Chick with a dick*."

I chuckled and told him my name.

We didn't kiss on our first date.

Having a twenty-four-year-old boyfriend at eighteen introduced me to a whole new world. He'd come to all of *spAnk*'s gigs and help us get our equipment set up—a true roadie. We'd take weekend trips to the beach. We went on a three-day hike through the Grampians, which was gruelling, but unforgettable and breathtaking, and took a ten-hour drive up to Mallacoota to celebrate the

---

18 Jumping forward in time, Serafeim's birthday is also the same as my mother's and his father was also a Pisces.

go

transition into the year 2000, where we went prawning in the moonlight. Kerry joined us. He taught me how to fish in Sandypoint. I caught a red snapper on my first go, but threw it back in the sea, much to his disappointment. We'd spend random nights together in the bush, with his mates drinking beer, and talking about music and cars. We'd cruise through the Dandenong Ranges in his Charger listening to albums from Magic Dirt, L7, Nightmares on Wax, and psychedelic metal bands like Gordian Knot.

I quickly fell in love with Craig. But I think, what I loved the most, was the freedom that came with the relationship.

Until I learnt about his condition.

One day, in late 2000, we were chilling out in bed in the bungalow in the backyard of his parents' house in Lilydale. I'd slept over, like I often did, after attending a party one of his mates had held the night before. Craig's face paled as he pushed on his right ribs, his eyes focussed on the ceiling. He jumped out of bed and turned on his PC and shook his knees up and down waiting for it to boot up. His impatience got the better of him and he snatched his black Ibanez Destroyer from the stand and played a few rapid scales and guitar solos. When the PC had booted up, he put the guitar down, pushed on his right ribs again and the PC froze. He moved the mouse from side to side trying to reactivate the cursor, but nothing happened.

"Fuck!" Craig slammed his fist on his desk and turned the computer off manually.

"Are you all right?" I said, rubbing some sleep out of my eyes.

Craig looked at me. His eyes squinted, and his neck craned inwards. He burped as if he was about to throw up, and pulled at the collar of his black Metallica t-shirt.

"You love me, don't you, Jess?"

"Yes. What's going on?" I sat up.

"But you're still young. You're going to change. You're going to want to be with other people."

"Craig, I love you. Things aren't going to change. I want to be with you," I said.

"I don't know what I'd do without you, Jess." Craig's voice squeaked and crackled on my name. He stood up and swayed backwards and forwards. He grabbed the back of the computer chair and lowered himself to the floor, pushing at his ribs and burping some more. His breathing was laboured, and he began to sweat. "I couldn't live without you, Jess. I couldn't. I wouldn't." Craig looked up at me with an expression of torture on his face.

I got out of bed and kneeled down beside him. I wasn't sure what was going on with his ribs, but the signs of an anxiety attack were a sure thing.

I rubbed his back and consoled him. Told him that I'd never leave him, that it was all going to be okay, until he calmed down and told me that he had a condition called Gilbert's Syndrome, a genetic liver disorder which caused fatigue, unusual patterns of anxiety, loss of appetite, nausea, abdominal pain, and loss of weight, among other symptoms.

I said, "Okay. It's okay."

Craig lay back down and slid a video cassette of the Simpsons into his ancient VHS player—a show he was obsessed with—in order to calm himself down.

I showered, listening to him chuckle and quote lines in sync with the characters. I dressed in my black tailored pants and white shirt for my night shift at Chapelli's Restaurant in Chapel Street, South Yarra, like it was just another day, thinking about what I was going to listen to during the sixty-minute drive into the city from Craig's. I gave him a quick kiss on the forehead, said I'd see him in a couple of days, and headed off.

I got into my Gemini, made my way to Maroondah Highway, and pushed my foot right down on the accelerator until I exceeded the eighty-kilometre-an-hour speed limit on the three-lane road. I turned the stereo up as loud as possible, rolled the windows down, and zoomed through every amber light belting out Magic Dirt's 'I Was Cruel' at the top of my lungs: *I'm sorry ... cruel, Forgot ... my shell ... head back in ... stick the knife in, When ya, when ya ... Tearing ... I was so cruel ...*

In a haze, on autopilot, I outran the traffic, weaving in and out of lanes, trying to get ahead of every single car I saw in front of me. This strange sense of focus, yet complete out of body experience, had me navigating the road like a race car driver.

Until another vehicle, going half the speed as me, cut me off.

I slammed my foot on the brake, lost control of the wheel, caught a tyre on the edge of the median strip, and spun the car round and round and round until I gave up trying to control it and yanked the handbrake on. I stalled in the centre of the highway. The horn of an oncoming truck gained volume. I lifted my gaze to the open window and was met with streaks of grey and heat gushing past my face. The truck's horn subsided like it was disappearing off the edge of a cliff. It missed colliding with my car by mere centimetres.

The little Italian woman who'd cut me off, got out of her car and ran over to me.

"Sorry, so sorry! You okay? I no see you. I so sorry, I no see you! You hurted? Your car? Okay? Sorry!"

I shook all over. Inside and out. My hands trembled

like my knuckles had been plucked out. I swallowed and nodded. Mentally scanned my body, head to toe, to see if I felt any pain anywhere. I was fine. And I would later find out my car was without a scratch.

"It's fine," I said, and turned the key in the ignition. It struggled to start the first few times, but when it chugged to life, the stereo restarted and Adalita's aggressive voice alarmed the woman. She stumbled backwards and into her car.

I practically *rolled* to the nearest exit in the left lane and pulled over at the side of a random street lined with eucalyptus trees. I allowed the car to stall without touching the ignition. The sun shone through my windscreen in such a way that I could see my reflection in the glass. We stared at each other, my reflection and I, taking long deep breaths, trying to calm the trembling.

Then I burst into tears. My body shook so hard it made the car squeak.

"Whyyyy?" I cried out, my voice croaking from the tears. "Fuck!"

I didn't run. Yet. My love for Craig, even though it was a borderline brotherly love, did trump the irrational burden I felt by his illness and anxiety. But it affected me subconsciously. Whenever he'd have an attack, I would feel myself retreating. Not physically, but in my head. During an attack it was as if I saw him through the narrow end of a paper trumpet. All the feelings surrounding the event went dark. I honed in on the moment. Got through it. And *then* let the paper trumpet uncurl.

In the summer transitioning between 2000 and 2001, I was nineteen going on twenty. I spent four weeks of it, over Christmas, vomiting. The doctor I saw didn't know what was wrong. He said it must have been a virus of some sort, and to come back in a couple of weeks if it persisted.

It did persist. My mum and I thought I had something serious that the doctors had never come across before, and therefore couldn't diagnose. All sorts of scenarios flicked through my mind. And I was scared.

I didn't want to be around Craig. I kept telling Mum to answer his phone calls and tell him I was asleep. The only person I would see was Kerry, who visited now and again to keep me company. Because I was feeling so ill and it was impossible to function like a normal human being, I lied to my boss at Chapelli's—told him I had an ovarian cyst and had to have an operation. I couldn't keep taking days off with the excuse of feeling nauseous. If it hadn't happened over summer, I'd have fallen behind in my studies too.

I sat on the front porch with Mum one day while experiencing a few minutes of relief. She'd made me some cauliflower soup again (imagine pumpkin soup made with cauliflower instead), which was all I seemed to be able to stomach. I sat in silence for a while, taking slow deep breaths to try and extend the relief for as long as possible, watching the grass sway in slow motion, listening to the birds chirp as if from afar and the muffled incomprehensible mess from the TV wafting through the living room window. We speculated on what could be wrong with me. Glandular fever? But why was I vomiting? Hepatitis? The doctor tested me for that. Abdominal tumour? Stress? Anxiety? But about what? I wasn't pregnant, we were sure of it. It was the first thing the doctor tested for, plus I hadn't missed a period.

The postie dropped mail into our mailbox. Mum smiled

jessica bell

and waved, then strode to the front of the lawn and retrieved a bunch of envelopes. By this time, Mum was completely off the drugs, but still experiencing withdrawal symptoms on and off. She often had days when she looked completely normal.[19]

"What's that?" Mum tossed an envelope in my lap. It was addressed to me. I shrugged and opened it.

As soon as I saw what it contained, I burst into tears and handed the piece of paper to Mum. She looked at it and cried out, "Oh my God. Oh my *God*." She held the paper to her head and muttered something I couldn't comprehend amidst stricken breath. It looked as though she was about to yell and scream. I wouldn't have blamed her. But she took a deep breath and stopped. She frowned with a sad pitiful smile, then held me in her arms, for what seemed like hours, and I bawled my eyes out into the nape of her neck.

"Let's go inside and talk about your options," she whispered. "You don't have much time."

I nodded and wiped away my tears with the heels of my palms.

I was approximately twelve weeks pregnant. The doctor had gotten the first test wrong. And in those days, it was rare for a doctor to sign off on an abortion if you were more than twelve weeks pregnant. I had to make a decision. Fast.

I told Craig the news over the phone and he insisted I come to his house and speak to his parents about it. I said I didn't want to speak to them, that I knew what I wanted.

"But Mum said she would help bring it up with us."

"I don't want your mother to bring it up."

"She wants you to keep it."

---

19 I later learnt that she had tried to hide her pain from me as much as possible; that being 'pain free' was the only way she felt we'd be able to rebuild our relationship.

go

"I don't." I sobbed.

"Please just come here so we can talk about this as a family."

"You're not my family," I snapped. "My family is here."

He continued to pester me, his tone void of warmth. His words echoing the voices of his parents in the background. I didn't have the energy to tell him how much it hurt that he couldn't speak for himself. I didn't have the energy to explain why I needed my mother more than him right now. I didn't have the energy to let him be a part of it, because I felt like I would be looking after him, when I needed someone to be looking after me. It would be a year before I left Craig, but I knew that we wouldn't be together forever. I didn't see him in my future. I wanted to be with a man who was healthy. I couldn't live the rest of my life being a cushion for panic attacks. And I was young enough to still be able to escape that. I had a choice. And I had to do what was best for *me*.

Run.

Run as fast as you can.

"I want to keep it," Craig said again, dragging out the vowels in each word like a whining child.

But my decision was made.

I blubbered something incomprehensible, hung up on him, and booked an appointment with a local GP to sign off on an abortion right away.

January, 2001, Demetri let Mum and I out of the white Beetle in front of the Royal Women's Hospital in Melbourne before finding a parking spot.

Because I was so far along in my pregnancy, I was required to go under a general anaesthetic.

Happy New Year.

My mother showed zero per cent fear and one hundred per cent emotional support for me. Though when I recently asked her about it, she said not only was she petrified, but the withdrawal was causing her strange nerve pains down her neck, and every time I'd touch her, it felt like razor blades touching her skin.

I was oblivious.

I suppose it's where I got my talent for hiding my feelings.

On the gurney in the theatre, the bright lights stung my eyes like admonitions as the surgical nurse covered my nose with an oxygen mask. Within seconds, the doctors' voices melted together then froze like Cottees Ice Magic to air.

When I woke up, two hours later than I was supposed to, I was told that I'd had a reaction to the anaesthetic and almost died.

I did not see any light. My unconscious world was as dark as my conscious one.

My energy levels being low, when I tried to walk, my legs would bend like pipe cleaners. Instead of walking out of the hospital like everyone else who had gone in for an abortion that day, I had to be pushed to the car in a wheelchair. Getting into the car was a chore. The ground gravitated towards my body and my joints felt like they'd been replaced with metal bolts.

At home, I slept for days. When I wasn't sleeping, I lay flat on my stomach, and despite my bed sheets feeling stiff and itchy, I gave into the weight of my body sinking into them. I drank sugar water, ate cauliflower soup and buttered toast. The thick air in my bedroom coursed through my mouth and lingered around my ears with a low hum. Every breath I'd take, I'd hear it, as if someone was next to me blowing into my hollow temples.

Until I woke up one morning like I'd just recovered from a very long hangover. I stared at my ceiling, trying to determine whether I still felt sick or not. I didn't. I smiled. And it dawned on me what I had just gone through.

Did I really just kill my baby?
Yes.
Am I sad about it?
Don't think so.
Am I sad about not being sad about it?
Uh ...

There was a knock at my door and it opened before I had a chance to speak. It was Craig. I never got a chance to finish the conversation with myself.

Craig sat on the edge of my bed. He leaned over and kissed me, stroked my breasts.

"They already feel smaller," he said.

I gritted my teeth, buried my face in my pillow, feigned a smile, and turned back around.

"I'm sorry about all this." I did my best to not seem cold and heartless.

Craig smiled, lay down, and spooned me. The musty smell of his bungalow mixed with car grease permeated the room. The arms wrapped around my body felt foreign.

I no longer belonged in his embrace.

A year later my parents got married, sold the house in Heidelberg, bought an apartment in Coburg, which I moved into, and shipped themselves off to Greece so that Mum had a more tranquil place to heal. I continued my Bachelor of Arts and worked as a waitress in Brunswick

Street, Fitzroy, in a café bar called The Hideout.[20] I studied and worked. Studied and worked. Until I wasn't able to ignore the voice of my reflection any longer.

The disconnect from Craig that I experienced after the abortion launched me back into a vicious self-destructive cycle. First, I pretended everything was okay. Ignored my feelings of inadequacy. Played house and happy single white female, despite not officially breaking up with Craig. It was all so fake, and deep down, I was convinced I was a bad person. That I would be better off not caring about myself, not bothering to act responsibly, because, you know, who gives a fuck if I have a fatal accident and die, right? Who is going to give a crap about a selfish cold-hearted baby killer like me who pushes people out of her life because they're *sick*?

But you've seen all this before, so ...

... let's fast forward through the following year of cheating on Craig because I couldn't muster the strength to tell him I didn't love him anymore until the guilt got the better of me and I finally did it in his bungalow and cried all the way home because, again, I didn't truly understand my own motives; and let's fast forward through the one night stands in toilet cubicles, the drunken nights dancing on bars and falling backwards into a display of glass bottles, the kissing of various women in nightclubs, the men I flirted with but never knew the names of, the passing out on random people's floors more times than I can count ... should I remind you about the self-loathing, the worthlessness, the total emotional chaos that this behaviour inflicted on me, and that I couldn't stop myself because I didn't feel loved, and I didn't believe I was worth loving, and I didn't believe I could ever let myself love someone again because I would just ... *abort* them?

---

20 The Hideout is now closed down.

go

Quick, let's get to the part about the cliff. I can't take this self-pity anymore.

It was the summer of 2002. I deferred Uni for a semester so I could have some fun (you know what fun means, right?) on Ithaca. I spent weeks, shit-faced to complete oblivion on tequila shots, every single night. I may need to remind you that Ithaca is a Greek island. There are sharp cliffs and windy pitch-black roads and other drunk drivers behaving irresponsibly.

I can't for the life of me remember how I got there. Maybe I'd hired a moped. Maybe it was the year I bought one. I can't remember. It's all a drunken blur. Was I even on a moped? Could I have been in someone's car and dropped off on the side of the road? Was I sleep walking? Taking a stroll? Stumbling home on foot because I couldn't find a lift?

I don't know.

All I remember is being on a road, and then suddenly being stunned into lucid consciousness by a horn and a sharp flash of someone's high beams, and when the blue memory of the light had dissipated from my vision, I was faced with ... open space.

I looked down and my feet were inches away from the edge of a cliff. I gasped. No. Did I gasp? Or was it silent shock, a pocket of air caught in my throat? One thing was for sure: the realization that if I stepped forward I could be a pulverized body on the shore of someone's private beach.

I lowered myself to the gravelly surface. I sat still, listening to the soothing distant whoosh of the sea brushing up against the shore, watching the glimmering moonlight on the water and the lights of a car crawling up the side of Cephalonia, the island opposite Ithaca. I couldn't remember *why* I was there, or *how* I got there, but I could *feel* I was there.

I lay on my back and the rapid beating of my heart slowed. I scraped my fingers through the gravel and picked up a few pebbles. I cupped and uncupped my fingers around them, each time digging the jagged edges into my palms with a little more force. I looked up to the sky and the cluster of stars above bounced around in my intoxicated vision. I shivered, my head throbbed, and my stomach gurgled.

I rolled over and threw up.

"What the fuck are you doing?" I whispered. "What the *fuck* ... are you doing to yourself?"

I didn't know.

But something had to change.

You've been thinking about not existing. No, you don't want to kill yourself, you said. You want to know what it feels like to not 'be'?

Of course, if you didn't exist, you wouldn't be able to feel what it's like, but let's imagine for a moment that you don't exist, and can actually experience not existing for the sake of it. I'll play along with you. We can do this together.

You imagine not existing would feel like a pleasant dream. Groan. *The kind where you are experiencing the dream, and watching yourself in the dream. You imagine there would be no pain, guilt, regret, heavy petting, or loneliness. You imagine the feeling of death, the release of worry—and the feeling of birth. The innocence of not knowing anything except the warmth of your mother's first embrace.*

go

You imagine not existing would be freedom. The ultimate freedom from the ever-increasing control and contradiction of being a responsible adult.

But there is no-one to share it with.

Because you don't exist.

You're me. And I'm you.

But only in the mirror.

My experience at the edge of the cliff was followed by a week of 'uncharacteristic' August rain. I stayed indoors and read books, listened to music, slept. I spent lazy evenings in front of the TV drinking the Lipton's tea Zacharati had been having shipped over from Australia for the previous twenty years.[21] I potted about the house. From bed to backyard, from couch to kitchen table, from back verandah to front porch. I took walks along dirt tracks thinking about returning home to an empty apartment, university lectures, and once again, to finding a job.

But I still had a month to go before I had to head back. All my summer 'friends' had left the island now, so I spent time with a cousin of mine, who was also visiting from Australia. One quiet night in late August, when the party season was well and truly over, my cousin and I went to the local bar for a drink. And let me emphasize that it was *a* drink.

We sat at the empty bar, sipping our vodka lemons, listening to the barman's sad attempt at clutching onto the party season as long as he possibly could by playing Men at Work's 'Down Under,' at full blast, for the millionth time that summer.

---

21 I never understood this as Lipton is available in Greece.

Though there were a handful of people sitting outside, no-one seemed drunk or in a party mood. No-one got up to dance.

Except one guy.

Hector. A typical dark, tall, solidly built young local, with big brown eyes, slick blonde hair, and a sharp clean-shaven jaw. We'd fooled around with each other earlier that summer, but never hung out long enough to develop any coherent emotional connection.

Originally sitting outside with his mates, he bolted inside and imitated the dance movements in the sand from the 'Down Under' music video—kicking his knees and legs up, waving his arms about, and then jumping about like a kangaroo. His mates called out, "*Ti kaneis re malaka? Trelos eisai!*" (What are you doing, man? You're crazy!) My cousin and I turned to watch, and laughed. Hector called out for his mates to join him, but no-one came, so he yanked me off my stool, spun me around, and lifted me off the ground.

He laughed like he had just been given the best news of his life and it charmed me.

What the hell?

Just go with it!

We pranced around like idiots, laughing, until the song changed. I said thanks for the dance, gave him a peck on each cheek, and sat back on my bar stool next to my cousin. She ordered another vodka. This time, I just had an Epsa Lemon (lemon soft drink).

To my surprise, Hector didn't sit back outside with his mates. He sat next to me.

"You're name is Tzessica, yes?" he said with a silky Greek accent.

I scoffed.

"Hector." He chuckled. "Nice to meet you." He winked,

go

clearly indicating jest. Of course he remembered who I was. But I don't think we'd ever officially told each other our names.

For a moment I was silent when he raised his hand for the barman's attention and ordered a bottle of Mythos beer. I wondered what horrible rumours he'd heard about me. To top off my own feelings of inadequacy, they were further consolidated that summer by circulating gossip that I was a slut, and that if anyone did as much as touch me, they'd probably catch AIDS.

When the barman gave Hector his beer, he said, "I just finished exams. No more high school. Cheers!" and clinked his bottle into mine.

I smiled and took a swig of my soft drink. "Cheers, Hector," I said, wondering why I'd never seen this innocent charm in him before. "Are you going to go to university?"

Hector nodded and grinned, opening his eyes wide. "I don't know which one yet. But yes. Somewhere on mainland."

"Cool." I thought he was very cute and wanted to hang out all night and chat. But he was younger than me. And the mental age difference between a nineteen-year-old sheltered male and a twenty-one-year-old well-travelled female is huge. I didn't want to go there.

I finished my soft drink and stood up. "I'm going home," I said, directing the comment to my cousin.

"Me too," she said, and slid off her bar stool.

I nodded at Hector, as a goodbye. It's a bit like a Greek version of tipping one's hat. Hector nodded back.

But right before I stepped out the door, Hector said, "See you here tomorrow night?"

I hesitated for a moment, and laughed.

And then said *yes*.

During the one month I had left on the island before embarking on a family trip to Germany, Hector and I spent a lot of time together. In the now quiet mornings, when the roads were wet with what I like to call patchwork rain (when it rains in one spot, but not a mere ten metres down the road) he'd come and pick me up from my grandparents' house on his blue and white *Papi*[22] and we'd ride to a café to play backgammon and drink Nescafé Frappé, sweet, with milk.

Life was good. Life was simple. Life was no longer a ten tonne cyberpunk fist trying to scratch its way into my chest.

Hector and I were so smitten with each other that I was already planning to move to Greece for him, and consequently give up on my music career. I just had to figure out how I could get back quicker than ten months when I would finish my degree.

Was I rushing into this? Hell yes. But I didn't care.

That rush of falling in love was back and it made my world a better place. I was not going to let go of this feeling if I didn't have to. Before I left, I gave him my favourite ring to remember me by. It was one I'd designed myself and had made especially on the island as a personal treat. It had a thick silver band with a groove along the centre of it. Along the groove were tiny inset gold balls. Hector having that ring was the only thing I felt would keep us connected when I was gone. It was the first possession in my life that represented a sentimental value, and I held onto that feeling for as long as possible.

The separation anxiety and love sickness I experienced

---

22 This is what an underbone motorcycle is called in Greece.

go

when I went to Germany with my parents, and Hector went off to college in Thessaloniki (Northern Greece), was ... if there is any appropriate word for it: theatrical. Mum and Demetri had taken me to Germany to see relatives I'd never met, and I spent the entire two weeks with a red face and a runny nose and a migraine from bawling and blubbering at the thought of never seeing Hector again.

The emptiness I felt without Hector was new.

It wasn't hopelessness, or loneliness.

It wasn't my usual depression in which I felt worthless, and it definitely didn't make me want to commit suicide.

This sadness was manic.

Like I was going through this torturous thing, *can't you see, can't you see, and why isn't anyone trying to help me find a solution? Why isn't anyone trying to help me get back to him?*

Imagine giving a homeless person a house, a night to sleep in a warm bed, and shower, and then saying, "Sorry, man, just kidding, you're stuck in the cold for life." The world had betrayed me. It teased me into submission and then pulled the ground from under my feet.

I wasn't going to stand by and let this happen to me. I was going to fight. Even if it meant crying in front of people I hardly knew and making a fool of myself.

Though at the time, I had no idea how I was going to cope with this gaping hole in my heart, I knew there would be light at the end of the tunnel. The problem was, I couldn't bring myself to be rational about it in order to calm down. I missed Hector. Missing Hector meant I'd never see him again. Never seeing him again meant he might as well be dead.

My life was over before it had begun.

Was *I* experiencing panic?

I wouldn't be surprised if these feelings were exacerbated, or in fact, directly linked to alcohol withdrawal. My reaction to the separation was not normal.

I returned to Melbourne in late October of 2002 and lived in my parents' apartment in Coburg. I had to pay rent so that my parents could afford to pay rent on Ithaca, but that was the least of my problems. I *needed* to get back to Greece to be with Hector, and I needed to get back fast.

As I was still deferred from Uni until the following February, I launched straight into finding work. I got a day job in a sandwich bar, and a night job in a pub, both in South Yarra. I worked six days and five nights a week, hoarding cash in my bedside table drawer, did grocery shopping and showered at three in the morning, ate on the go, and rarely saw my friends. I can't remember a single day I spent with Kerry in which I wasn't daydreaming about being back in Greece with Hector. I even found a way to finish the last semester of my degree in Greece via correspondence. I transferred to Deakin where they had a distance education program.

I was on a mission to abandon my life in Australia and start anew with a young man I believed to be the best thing that had ever happened to me. And I was confident I knew what I was doing, because I hardly drank. My head was screwed on straight. Right?

It wasn't. Because I was drunk on love.

About a month after I'd returned home, I started getting text messages from Hector asking things like, "How many people did you sleep with during the summer?" To that question I lied and said only him. 1) Because I didn't think it was any of his business, and why should it

go

matter how many people I'd slept with for us to love each other? 2) I was ashamed of my behaviour and deep down I *felt* like a slut. I couldn't allow that guilt to rule my life so lying about it seemed the best way to tame it. 3) It was a reflex. It was how I ran from negative emotion. We all know how good at that I had become.

When I'd answer his questions, he'd text back with rumours he'd heard and ask if they were true.

For example: Did you have a threesome with so and so in the football field? Did you dance naked on the bar? Did you give so and so a head job in front of so and so? Do you have AIDS? *Do you, did you, do you, did you ...*

None of it was true.

I told him so. I told him I danced a lot. I told him I flirted a lot. I also told him that there was nothing wrong with a girl having some fun, even though the text interrogations made me feel like there was something *very* wrong with a girl having some fun.

I felt physically ill.

Then he broke up with me via text message.

I begged him to take me back via text message.

He took me back via text message.

We declared our love for each other, once more, via text message.

Then I started getting texts accusing me of being a liar. I'd done this, but said that, I'd said that, but done this. *No, no, no!* Okay, I lied about how many people I'd slept with. But that was it. I wondered whether I should just come clean.

But I couldn't. I thought he would split up with me for good. My life would be over if he did that. So I sat on the lie.

Then he split up with me for thinking I was lying about more rumours. He told me his friends were telling him I was bad news. One of them told him I was a prostitute in Australia.

He split up with me again.

Via text.

I begged him to take me back again, pleaded my case. Insisted I was telling the truth.

His silence killed me and I cried all night and got to work the next day an emotional wreck with another migraine.

I checked my phone every five minutes, a tissue permanently in my hand.

Until he finally texted ... an answer for all twenty-five of my unanswered pleas.

Yes, he would take me back, on the condition that I promised him on my mother's life that I was not lying to him.

My heart beat in my ears. *I had lied, I had lied, I had lied ... but not about what he thought I'd lied about.*

I promise on my mother's life I have not lied to you.

We got back together. Via text.

As it turns out, being drunk on love is just as bad, if not worse, than alcohol. It blurred my vision of all the signs that Hector may not be good for me after all. I completely ignored the voice of my reflection, who, for once, was trying to save me not sabotage me.

It's not a good idea to uproot your whole life for him.
But I've already made the decision.
Unmake it.
But I've already quit the band.
Unquit it.
You can't move halfway across the world for him.
But I've already told my parents I'm coming.
Untell them.
I've already put the paperwork through for my work permit.

So what? He's too young. And jealous. This isn't going to end well.

It will get better. Once he sees me again he'll forget all about the rumours.

The rumours that circulated during that last trip to Ithaca, would not only be the ultimate bane of my three-year relationship with Hector, but they left a bad taste in my *own* mouth with regards to the island.

It was no longer paradise. It was hell.

And when I moved there, I became a recluse.

I returned to Greece in February of 2003, one week before my 22nd birthday. When I arrived, I jumped straight on a bus to Thessaloniki to see Hector. I wanted to stay longer, but his parents insisted I would disrupt his study routine, and asked that I return to Ithaca and wait for him to visit in four weeks' time during Carnival on March 18.

I respected their wishes, and did what I was told like a good little Greek girl. But inside I was fuming. I wasn't used to being told what to do anymore, and my actions being determined by someone *else's* parents was even worse. I was an adult. But Hector was not.

As the visit was only a few days long, Hector did not broach the subject of my reputation. But every single second, I was waiting for it. I walked on egg shells, and from moment to moment they'd crackle in my head.

I returned to Ithaca to live with my parents with the intention of moving to Athens when I finished my degree and to then look for a job teaching English as a foreign language. I worked at Spavento as a waitress, a café bar situated by the water (which I once fell into with a tray of milkshakes) in Kioni, owned by Demetri's sister and her husband, and a crêperie in Vathi, owned by Demetri's sister's husband's brother.

I didn't drink. I didn't party. I became a complete opposite of myself to try and prove, to Hector (and the general population of Ithaca and perhaps even myself), that I was not the person everyone thought I was.

I'd study. I'd work. I'd come home—a 'basement' level living area of a two-storey (very damp) house with a very low ceiling my parents were temporarily renting.

I'd spend hours deflecting accusatory texts from Hector, then lock myself in my bedroom and read books. Lots of books. Everything under the sun by Margaret Atwood, and random titles borrowed from Demetri's sister by authors such as Ruth Rendell, Simone de Beauvoir, and Germaine Greer. I listened to pirated CDs purchased from African American nomads that drifted through the Greek islands selling them: Beck, Madonna, No Doubt, Eminem, Kate Bush, Norah Jones, Radiohead, and Black Eyed Peas were on constant repeat.

I was lonely. Very lonely. I cried, every day, 'looking forward' to the days Hector would come back from Thessaloniki to visit his family. What was I looking forward to? Manipulative emotional abuse? Clearly I was not right in the head. I wanted nothing more than to make my own way in the world, but I couldn't. I needed a residency permit to live and work in Greece legally.

But according to the Greek legislation:

I couldn't get a residency permit without valid health insurance.

I couldn't get health insurance without a legal job.

I couldn't get a legal job without a residency permit.

Two years we spent trying to solve this problem. And I couldn't leave the island in case the cops picked me up

go

and deported me back to Australia. Thankfully my family made an agreement with the police: as long as I stayed on the island, they'd turn a blind eye until we sorted it out. But *I* couldn't turn a blind eye to my situation: I was a young woman in my early twenties with a passion for music and words, living in isolation from the real world.

I went bat crazy.

The only person who saved me from imploding was my mother.

One day when I was couped up in my room reading, she knocked on my door, waited for me to speak, and then entered.

"What are you doing?" She leant into the door frame and pushed her glasses up her nose.

I lifted *Alias Grace* by Margaret Atwood in the air and shook it.

"You need to do something else. You need to take control. You can't keep sitting in here all day," she said.

I puckered my brow, wondering what the fuck it was I was supposed to do, given the circumstances.

"You haven't written a song in ages."

I stared at her. The last thing I wanted to do was write music. It would only remind me about everything I had given up.

"Look. Why don't you write an album? I'll record it for you on the computer. We still have some music contacts here. We can send demos out. And when you eventually get to Athens you can start playing solo gigs there."

I didn't answer. I had gotten so used to not speaking that it felt like a waste of time to even try.

Mum stepped out of the room and came back in with Demetri's Les Paul electric guitar. She leaned it against the wall.

"Just write and record one song. If you still don't want to do it after that, then I'll accept it. But I can't stand by and watch you waste away. You're too talented, Juice."

"But I—"

"One song. For me?"

I nodded. Mum closed the door. I picked up the guitar. And suddenly I was home.

The long-awaited collision of my fingers and brain caused a mass explosion of catchy guitar riffs and clever evocative lyrics. And a couple of weeks later I had an album. I called it *Ash11*. Ash being representative of the Phoenix, and the number 11 a symbol of balance between the spiritual and material world.[23]

Putting my heart and soul back into music, however, was merely a painkiller, not a cure. And instead of motivating me to continue pursuing a career in music when I would eventually leave the island for the big city, it further consolidated the fact that I was *trapped*. My future, at this point, a complete unknown.

Everything seemed hopeless.

And Hector's behaviour hadn't even reached its peak.

Summer, Ithaca, 2004. A red moon reflected anger and unfounded jealousy across Frikes bay. Motionless, I stared at Hector as he flung his arms around and screamed. His voice boomed like a nuclear bomb—so loud it was silent. Dark blue and white waves crashed against the rocks surrounding the pier as my heart melted into a mass of hardened black oil. Hector yanked the ring I'd given him off his little finger.

"You're a liar," he hissed, and flung the ring so far that

---

[23] You can listen to the entire album on Bandcamp, here: *bit.ly/JessicaBell1*

go

it disappeared from sight before sinking to the bottom of the sea.

I cried. I cried so hard my chest and ribs ached. After all these years of messing with people's hearts, Hector was now doing the very same thing to me. Over and over and over again. Was the universe calling for payback?

"I'm not lying! Why do you keep doing this to me?" I sobbed.

"You *smiled* at him." Hector spun around to face me and slapped his hands on his head.

"I don't even know who you're talking about," I cried. "I was smiling towards the entrance. Where else am I supposed to look? My feet?"

"Liar!"

"I'm not lying!" I squatted in the middle of the road with a moan, trying to catch my breath, watching my tears splatter on the asphalt and blend into the roughness of the black surface. I could hardly recognize myself. This crying. It would not stop, and the ache that came with it was ripping me apart so violently I was ready to jump into my parents' car and drive myself off a cliff.

"You're a slut. It's over. I mean it this time."

Hector may have meant it, but it didn't last long. He took me back the next day. And broke up with me again the day after that, and then took me back again. And I let it happen. I would let it happen at least twenty more times in 2004 alone.

Because I promised myself, I would *not abort*.

I'd convinced myself it was time to stop running.

The only time I should have.

It reached -8 degrees Celsius on Ithaca in December of 2004, and snowed—a rare occurrence on a Greek island—

when I thought I had well and truly fucked up my life for good.

I stepped outside, hugged my coat around my body, and flipped myself forward to swing the hood over my head.

Wouldn't it be great to catch pneumonia and die?

Mum had asked me to buy her some cigarettes from the Zacharoplasteio (a delicatessen that doubled as a café-bar). Begged, more like it. It was very hard to get me to do anything those days without a back and forth verbal struggle.

As I walked down the unevenly concreted road, I focussed on my feet. The gravel rolling beneath my soles contrasted nicely with the winter hum of the abandoned village and, for a moment, I enjoyed the solitude.

I stopped and looked up at the dark sky. Light snow floated towards the earth creating a layer of grey-blue mist in the valley. All I wanted right then and there was for Hector to visit. To stand there together, listening to our hearts beat in unison to the breath of the night. But I also knew, in reality, there was no way Hector would stand in the middle of a road to take pleasure in a moment of still life. But as I said, I was devoted. I would not cheat or renege on my commitment. I would love him no matter how hard things got. I might as well have been addicted to cutting myself. Essentially, that's what I was doing by staying with him.

The bright lights of an oncoming car startled me, and I quickly regained momentum, being sure to keep my eyes focussed on my feet. I wasn't going to risk making eye-contact with another man should it be the catalyst of another rumour to further consolidate my 'sluttiness.' I couldn't handle another break-up. I'd lost count now of how many times it had happened. And despite it only taking a couple of hours for us to get back together most of the time, each time it happened, it was more traumatic than the last. I always assumed it would be the final time, and I would be well and truly alone, on a Greek island in winter, when no-one was there except aged locals, stuck in a dungeon with a mother who was struggling with her own demons, and a father who hardly spoke, and my reflection, who found an opportunity during every waking moment to make me feel like a total waste of space.

When I entered the Zacharoplasteio, the men drinking beer and smoking at the bar all spun their heads in my direction. Their hidden smirks rattled my bones. I accidentally caught the eye of a local shepherd and quickly looked away when I realized who it was. He'd apparently been spreading rumours that he'd slept with my mother and me. Together. Fear shot through me at the thought that all the men in that place would now take this as a sign it was true. I grabbed a few packets of Silk Cut for my mother and hurried home, crying, wondering whether I should give up on this whole thing, give up on Hector, go home to Australia and never come back. I was ready to break my promise. And that alone devastated me. I'd let myself down.

That night, I locked myself in my bedroom, again. But instead of reading a novel, I started, without really knowing what I was doing, writing one.

My first novel.

It was about Hector. Ithaca. Loneliness. Hate.

When I read it back to myself, I despised the character I'd based on myself. She was deceitful, selfish, openly hurtful to others, a bitter gossip, cold-hearted, judgemental, and she'd demean others at the drop of a hat without taking a single moment to consider their feelings.

My stomach sank.

Who am I?
How have I become this person?
How is it possible that I have all these evil thoughts?
That's not me. It can't be!

I removed myself from my computer and sat in the bathroom in front of the mirror.

"I don't like you," I said to my reflection. "I don't like you at all."

After weeks of trying to fix myself in the book, I realized I wasn't fixable.

The only solution was to hit delete.

And start again.

In late 2004, I received my residency permit. As far as I know, the health insurance company was 'persuaded' to give me insurance, so I could be legally hired at Spavento (my aunt and uncle's café-bar in a little village named Kioni), so I could legally apply for a residency permit.

I bow to the undersides of tables.

I very quickly went on the hunt for a job. I found *one* that I was interested in applying for. An editorial position at a company called New Editions which published English Language Teaching course books.

I sent in my application, and was called in for an interview. I needed to be in Athens for the interview in two weeks. So on sheer determination and faith that I could turn my life around on 1000 Euros worth of savings—and some luck I believed I was bound to be owed by now—I packed my bags and shipped myself off to Athens without having a place to live. Thankfully a family friend put me up for a couple of weeks while I looked for an apartment. I found one, paid 700 Euros for the bond and the first month's rent, and prayed I had the job in the bag.

go

On the morning of my interview, the December winter sun warmed my hands as I waited on a bench by the seaside in Paleio Faliro. In thirty minutes I had to be at New Editions. High on perceived freedom and hope, I convinced myself that I would get this job, and then I would have money to catch a train to Thessaloniki every weekend to see Hector. I believed that seeing him every weekend would change everything as I'd be able to divert him from being so influenced by what others said.

Everything is slipping into place.

I ate breakfast on the bench and checked the time on my phone more times than the traffic lights at the nearby intersection changed. The voices of Greek gossiping women in passing muffled as I tried to focus on the sound of the waves behind me. I needed to relax. My palms sweated and I felt like I was breaking out in a rash, itchy and burning all over my face and neck. I prayed I wasn't going all red and blotchy from the cold. I wanted this job more than anything. I couldn't go back to the island. Not now. Not now I'd finally got off.

It took me fifteen minutes to walk to New Editions from my new apartment and I waited for about five minutes before I was summoned in.

Behind a desk sat a handsome olive-skinned man in an expensive suit. He stood and shook my hand.

"Jessica. Nice to meet you. I'm Simon. Please, take a seat." His South African accent was rather toned down to what I'd been used to hearing from the South African expats I'd met on Ithaca. He gestured towards two women, Pat and Denise, who I assumed were also editors at the company, and introduced me to them too. Pat was freckled and voluptuous, dressed all in black, and had a very strong Irish accent. Denise looked a lot like Princess

Diana, with the exact same eyes and shyness about her too. I wasn't too sure about her. She seemed to literally have a stiff upper lip. (Though she turned out to be a really lovely woman.) I smiled and shook their hands before being seated.

The interview went pretty quickly, and I hardly remember saying a thing while Simon recited my resume and annotated it aloud. Pat and Denise were taking notes, glancing at me now and again as if they were peering above glasses. I was then asked to take a test—to edit a sample from one of their books.

I wasn't sure I'd done very well, having never professionally edited a thing before in my life, and my hope began to subside. I'd already mentally prepared to scour through the classifieds as soon as I got back to my apartment, when Simon said, "So you're a singer."

I nodded and smiled politely. For a moment I thought it was just going to be another one of those "My cousin lives in Australia, maybe he's heard of you" type conversations. Then he said, "We're looking for a young woman to sing and do some voice acting on the companion CD of the current course we're producing. Would you be interested?"

What the hell! Give it a go! Maybe there's a bit of cash in it ...

"Sure," I said. "What do you need me to do?"

Simon leaned back in his chair with a look of triumph on his face. He paused a moment, leaned forward on his desk, and clasped his hands together.

"I'll tell you what," he said. "You come into the studio for free, and we'll give you a three-month trial as an assistant editor. If you're a fast learner, and we see you are doing well, we'll offer you a permanent contract. If not, then neither of us lose."

go

I tried not to grin so wide, I really did, when I held out my hand for him to shake on it. "Deal," I said.

I did the recording. And I passed the three-month trial with flying colours. And now I have a career in both editing *and* voice acting.

Sometimes hardship leads to goodness. Every day of my life, I have to remind myself of this. I have to remind myself to stop listening to my reflection declare her insecurities and scepticism. Because no matter what I do, she will always be there, even when I think she's gone for good.

I am lucky.

I *am* lucky.

I'm lucky and you know it, clap your hands.

I awoke, startled, thinking I'd slept in and was late for work, when I realized it was the weekend. My first weekend after my first week at New Editions in January of 2005.

I got up to make coffee, squinting at my reflection in the mirror wall that covered the length of my thirty-two square metre apartment. In my kitchenette, I opened the mini fridge slotted neatly into a space below the sink. There was nothing to eat except lentil soup. There was no milk left for my coffee. I skipped breakfast and drank my coffee black, pretending not to wince because ...[24]

Sometimes hardship leads to goodness. Every day of my life, I have to remind myself of this.

I stepped onto the tiny balcony and smiled. I did it. I was here. Right where I had wanted to be since Laurel

---

[24] Random fact—I would eventually discover that milk makes me sick. I now drink my coffee black with a teaspoon of honey. It's actually really nice. You should give it a go!

died. A free independent woman. In that moment, it didn't matter that I hadn't become a rock star. What mattered was that I had got there myself and I had set aside the self-hatred.

I flicked through the possibilities of the day in my head.

You could spend some time wandering around Plaka ...

Or head down the coast to explore Glyfada.

Or grab a notebook and start writing ideas for a new novel.

On that note, next week, see if there are any writing opportunities at work.

You could do some writing in one of their course books. Get yourself in print.

Now that would be exciting. I could be a writer. A real published writer.

I took the last sip of my coffee and decided to get ready to explore the city. I then realized I had no clean underwear. Or clothes, in general. And my apartment didn't have a washing machine. And there wasn't a Laundromat in my neighbourhood either. I looked in my tattered black leather wallet. I had thirty Euros cash to my name, and I hadn't been paid my first monthly salary yet. I wouldn't be paid until the following month.

I opened the fridge to check if there really was only lentil soup left.

Yup.

I opened my cupboards to see if I had any cans of tuna or packets of pasta.

Nope. But ... crackers.

That's okay. Ration the lentil soup and eat it until it's finished, ration the crackers for breakfast so they last the week. Learn to drink your coffee black, go to the supermarket and buy whatever is the cheapest and will last the longest. Hang around at home and wash your clothes by hand in the bottom of the shower, and hang them to dry ... where?

Oh God ...

Not only did I not own a clothes horse, but I didn't have soap.

I sat on the edge of my bed with my legs crossed, facing the mirror wall. I looked at myself, smiled, and twirled a piece of my waist length auburn hair around my finger, then let it drop over my pale cheek. It retained a slight wave, and I thought I should buy some mousse when I could afford it.

Just put your hair in braids and leave them in over the weekend. Money saved. On Monday morning, your hair will be perfect. Gotta look good in the office.

I shivered, and realized I'd left the balcony door open a touch. I reached towards the heating dial, but paused mid-air.

No. Just lie in bed. Under the doona. Watch trashy MTV.

"It's not all that bad," I said aloud to my reflection, with a smile and a nod. "We spent the last two years holed up in a tiny bedroom, what's another month?"

In March, 2005, as soon as I got my first paycheck, I visited Hector in Thessaloniki. It was the first time I'd seen him since Christmas. He lay sideways on his bed watching TV. His clothes were strewn all over the place and his dirty wet footprints created a trail from the bathroom to his wardrobe. I stood in his kitchenette, checking if the pasta had boiled. I hooked a strand of extra thin spaghetti with a fork and lifted it out of the water, the whoosh of the oven fan supplementing the backing track of light traffic on wet roads.

I turned off the stove and the fan, gave the Napolitano sauce a stir, and drained the spaghetti in the colander.

"It's ready, come get it," I said in Greek. With his gaze glued to the TV screen, Hector nodded once, as if punctuating the end of a sentence, and dragged his feet to the table. My heart started to beat a little faster, wondering what I'd done wrong now. I pretended everything was fine, and placed his meal in front of him.

He didn't say thank you, but averted his gaze to his food.

"What's wrong?" I asked, and then took a mouthful of food to try and stop myself from crying. I could feel another accusation coming on. He jutted his head upward—the Greek gesture for 'no'—in this case meaning 'nothing'—but didn't look me in the eye. He twirled the pasta round his fork, using the aid of a spoon, something I never did. Watching him eat like that made me feel like a slob, so I got a spoon for myself too and mimicked the procedure. When I sat back down, Hector's chewing slowed down and the expression on his face turned sour.

"What is it?" I asked, with a slight tremor in my voice.

"You didn't mix butter into the pasta," he said, half whispering.

"Was I supposed to?" I rested my cutlery on the table with trembling hands. "I'll get you another serving with butter in it. Hang on."

Shaking, I reached for his bowl, but he snatched it up with one hand and hurled it at the wall right beside us. I flinched and buckled forwards as the plate shattered into pieces and pasta flew left, right, and centre, including all over my clothes.

I stood in silence, heart beating overtime in my ears, knees becoming weak, watching Hector's chest heaving and his fists clenching.

go

"You're a cheater," he spat. "You lie. You always lie."

I sank into my chair by the table and covered my eyes with my hands. I couldn't stop the tears. I couldn't stop Hector's deluded jealously. I decided then and there that this had to be it. I was leaving him. I couldn't cope with it a second more.

You're better than this.
You're a good person.
Am I? Am I really?

I stood up and brushed the pasta off my clothes with a tea towel, tears streaming down my cheeks. Hector kept the accusations of infidelity coming, pushed me to the ground, and ripped all his photos of me into tiny pieces in front of my face. But I blocked everything out with her voice as I packed my bag. I could feel her inside me, finally giving me the strength to do what I should have done a lot sooner, but in a way that was not damaging to myself.

As I was about to walk out the door, with my backpack slung over one shoulder, Hector said, "There's no bus tonight."

I paused and dropped my bag, wondering if there was a hotel close by I could stay in. But I didn't have any money for a hotel.

I was stuck.

Until morning.

I decided to give him one more chance ... and my reflection fell silent.

It was not characteristic of you to be so tactful. I was expecting you to swear at me, to tell me to tell him to go fuck himself, that I was an idiot for staying, but I suppose, I was growing up, and therefore, so were you.

Were you becoming a good person then? Or were you just being yourself? Were you struggling to understand yourself, to believe in yourself, to love yourself, too?

Had I misunderstood who you were all those years? Perhaps you weren't really the bad side of me after all. Perhaps you were just striving to find your voice in this world, like I'd been striving to find my place.

Did you understand how hard it was to leave him? Were you cutting me some slack? Were you training me so I'd be ready to live without you in the future? Without alcohol as a vice?

Had you let go of me that night, or had I let go of you?

Ithaca, August 15, 2005. I sat at the end of the bar in Frikes Bay. Hector was there for the summer holidays working as a barman, but as I only had two weeks off from work, this was my last day. The next day I would head back to Athens; back to the nine-to-five job that seemed to be the only thing keeping my head on straight.

I sipped my vodka lemon, being careful not to look at any men. I stared behind the bar, keeping my focus on Hector as he flirted with all the ladies ordering drinks. Sometimes I stared at my hands, clasping my glass. I drank too much, but this time it wasn't to numb myself, it was because I didn't know what to do with my hands and I didn't smoke and I couldn't look *any*where. I had to get through the night without another fight and five-minute break-up. Because I knew, that the next time it happened, it would be it.

I couldn't afford to fall apart. Not now.

I looked into my lap when Men at Work's 'Down Under' started to play. Again. All the skippers sang along,

go

holding their drinks in the air, toasting to Hector. He nodded at them, downed a shot, and launched into the 'Down Under' dance moves which originally charmed me to him. The girls he'd been serving giggled and wriggled, and pushed their chests forwards when they ordered more drinks. Hector winked, and tipped his head as a 'You're welcome,' with every drink he served. I wasn't jealous. I was frightened. Frightened he would momentarily slip out of his party animal skin and look at me when my eyes might accidentally glance past a man's face. He'd assume I was engaging in some sort of unspoken communication with him about a fictional affair.

Well.

It *did* happen.

Hector exited the bar, grabbed me by the arm, and dragged me behind the building through the staff area.

"Why did you smile at him?" he snapped, digging his fingers into my arm.

"At who? I wasn't smiling at anyone!"

"Don't lie to me. You were."

"Why aren't I allowed to smile?" My voice wavered. I shouldn't have been scared, but I'd spent the last three years in a constant fearful state that my body reacted that way without registering it.

"We're finished," he said with a nod. "I promise. This is it. This time is the last time." With a curled lip, he shoved me backwards as if I were rotten goods, and left me standing in the back alley. I leaned against the bright yellow wall, closed my eyes, and took a deep breath. I needed my reflection to tell me to be strong. To be strong and single. That I didn't need him in my life. That this was an opportunity to grow, to become a writer, a rock star, a person worth loving.

To start my own *real* life.

But she was gone.

I texted Hector over and over on my way back to Athens the next day, begging him, trying to explain I had not been unfaithful. But he didn't respond. Not the next day, or the day after that, or the day after that.

For the first time ever, he didn't respond to my pleas.

I'd love to say the choice of breaking up was completely mine. That I was strong. That I had left him myself. But it wasn't like that. Life is just not like that. Sometimes you get the things you need without making them happen yourself. Deep down I knew breaking up was for the best, and I took some consolation in the fact that I had stuck this relationship out, right until the very end. I didn't cheat, I didn't run, I didn't abuse alcohol, I didn't drive off a cliff.

But I *did* hate myself.

I cried so much.

I was so alone, and empty, and the saddest I had ever been.

I had no friends. Except for maybe one. Jenny Heath, a work colleague who I would eventually call my best friend. I emailed her to tell her what had happened, but I wasn't ready to bawl my eyes out in front of her yet.

But when I went into work the following Monday, Jenny handed me a gift-wrapped box. Everyone in the office had chipped in a few Euros to buy me a DVD player.

"Now you can distract yourself," she said, and gave me a big strong hug.

All my work colleagues got out of their seats, hugged me, and offered me words of encouragement.

"A beautiful, smart, and intelligent young woman like you doesn't need a dirt bag like that," said one. "He didn't

go

have a clue how lucky he was. Fuck him," said another. "I'll beat him up for ya," said a third with a wink.

I cried more. Of course I cried. Much to my embarrassment.

But for once in my life, they were happy tears.

The DVD player didn't stop me from texting Hector, and his continued silence ripped my heart out more and more each and every night I'd lie down to sleep.

There wasn't a single person I knew who I felt comfortable being a blubbering mess around. But if I'd kept trying to deal with it alone, holding my shit together, would have been a short-lived experience.

The only choice I had was to call my mother.

I pushed aside my reluctance to show my weakness, and dialled her number.

When she picked up the phone, the only words I could force from my lips amidst the heaving and sobbing were, "I need you."

Mum and Demetri dropped everything, and by the following weekend, they were at my apartment. They didn't try to reason with me and tell me to stop crying. They didn't tell me I was overreacting, or use clichés like 'time heals all wounds.' They didn't force me to talk, when I didn't want to talk. Instead, they did what I could not muster the strength to do myself.

They cleaned every nook and cranny of my apartment, did my laundry, filled my fridge and cupboards with food, treated me to take-away pizza, souvlakia, big blocks of chocolate, and replenished my empty bank account with a small injection of funds.

We spent time wandering around the Plaka and

Monastiraki, talking about nothing in particular, and being comfortable in each other's silence.

On the Sunday evening before my parents had to head back to Ithaca, we sat down for a meal in Thissio. As we waited for our food to come, Mum took my hand and squeezed it with a tentative smile.

"Do you want to start playing gigs again?" Mum asked.

I shrugged. "I guess it'd be fun."

"Foti, Mikhail's cousin, has a band here. He could probably help you."

"Okay." I nodded, void of enthusiasm. I didn't know how to be that person again. I didn't even know how to want it.

After a few moments of silence, Mum said, "Whatever it is you decide to do with your life, I'm already so proud of you, you know."

I blushed and swallowed the instinct to roll my eyes.

Demetri nodded. "I am too, Jessie. Very much so."

I laughed nervously, unable to fully grasp what was happening.

It was the beginning of our adult relationship.

The beginning of forgiveness and understanding.

And seeing my parents' love for what it had always been: unconditional.

part five
2005-2016

part five
2005–2016

go

October 2005, Athens. I sat on Foti's couch, guitar hooked under my right arm, plectrum slipping side to side in my sweaty pinch, waiting to audition. Foti, the family friend, led a band named *Frank*[25] and invited me to be the solo supporting act for one of his shows. In his enthusiastic reaction to my music, he told me I could be 'big.' But to get big I needed to meet an acquaintance of his, a music events manager he'd recently started collaborating with.

The buzzer rang.

"*Ella. Anigw.*" Foti pressed a button on the wall which opened the front door to the apartment building. I heard heavy footsteps echo through the stairway, then a deep velvety voice as Foti greeted this acquaintance of his.

My breath caught in my throat. This was it. My chance to do something with my music. I didn't want to blow it.

"Hi, my name is Serafeim," the events manager said in a thick Greek accent as he walked into the living room. "Foti tells me I *must* to hear you sing." I laughed nervously at the juxtaposition of his cute broken English and tough-guy exterior. I motioned to stand and shake his hand, but he insisted I stay seated. His thick black leather motorcycle jacket with shiny silver zips creaked as he sat down opposite me. His crystal eyes kept changing colour depending on which direction he glanced. I couldn't tell if they were grey, blue, or green, in the dimmed orange light. One thing was for certain—they were mesmerizing.

He crossed his legs, looked at my feet and smiled. "Army boots."

"You don't like them?" I said, unsure if that was the right thing to say or not.

"They're cool." He nodded his shaved head to indicate that I should start playing.

I cleared my throat and launched into my cover of 'Wonderwall,' by Oasis, before playing him one of my original songs. I didn't want to play covers, but Foti insisted I show Serafeim I was versatile and able to satisfy a Greek crowd thirsty for entertainment. I didn't want to be an entertainer. I wanted to be a rock star. I wanted to break hearts with my music. But at that point, as it had been so long since I'd dropped music, and hardly had a leg to stand on, I was willing to do whatever it took to get my foot back in the door.

Even a Greek one.

We sat in silence for a few moments after I finished my last song. Serafeim stared at me with an odd half-squint as if he was trying to size me up. It made me feel extremely uncomfortable in an oddly arousing way. I stared back, determined not to retreat like a nervous little girl.

His eyes were definitely blue. Exactly like Celestite Druze—light blue crystal.

Foti broke the silence. "What do you think?" he said, pushing his glasses up his nose and parking his butt on the armrest of the sofa I was sitting on. "She's great, isn't she?"

Serafeim nodded. Either he wasn't that impressed, or he was playing cool on purpose. *"Nai. Kali einai."*

Foti took Serafeim's smooth agreement as an opportunity to blabber on and on about me, and how he'd like me to be his support act at all their shows, and that Serafeim should collaborate with me too. At least that's what I thought I understood amongst his unrelentingly speedy Greek speech.

I watched as they spoke, desperate to contribute to the conversation, but unable to find the right words in Greek. I must have looked like a confused child.

My stomach was a mess. Nerves, excitement—the oddest feeling that I was doing something naughty by just sitting there, and that Mum would walk in at any moment and tell me to go to my room.

"Where you live?" Serafeim said. It took a moment to realize he was talking to me, and I stammered a bit.

"Paleio Faliro."

"I ride you. Come."

There's no denying that I accepted his offer.

Soon, in more ways than one.

A week later Serafeim took me along to see a Greek rock band at Underworld Club near Omonia Square—a band he said would be ideal for me to support at a forthcoming gig. On our return, I wrapped my arms around Serafeim's waist as the rumble of his motorcycle vibrated through my legs. The Athens autumn evening air was injected with the scent of his leather jacket and woody aftershave. Horns tooted in the near distance and engines growled when the lights turned green. I moved my face as close as I could to the back of his head and imagined what it would feel like to touch my lips to his skin.

The wind flicked my long black hair into the air and roared in my ears. "Hold on tight," he said, and secured my arms a little more around his waist.

I didn't let go until we arrived at my apartment.

I got off his 2005 Yamaha FZ1, the semi-suburban silence unequivocally more deafening than the city centre hum. He turned off the engine and looked me up and down.

"Thanks for the lift," I said, with a nervous smile. I reached in to kiss his left cheek, and then the right, as Greeks do when they say hello and goodbye. But he attempted to kiss me on the lips. I backed up and gasped.

As far as I was concerned, we were building a professional relationship, so I wasn't even going to go there.

"What are you doing?" I was confused. Had I given off the wrong kind of signal? Was my attraction for him that clear?

"Trying to kiss you."

"I—I just want to be friends." I didn't. I was worried that I was 1) ruining my chances, yet again, at doing something with my music, and 2) going to jump into a new relationship too quickly after Hector. I still had some soul searching to do and I needed to do that alone.

Serafeim nodded with a smooth smile. "Okay." He started the engine and rode away. I stared at the edge of the curb where his motorbike stood less than two seconds before. I looked up at the street light and watched the bugs fly in and out and around the lamp, the sound of cars from the highway a few blocks down purring seductively.

You should have kissed him.
He left so abruptly. Did I embarrass him?

I fumbled for my keys and bolted up three flights of stairs to my apartment. I had no idea why I was running. I threw my bag on my bed, locked myself in the bathroom.

You live alone. What are you doing?

I stared at myself in my mirror. White, with pink lips, and deep grey shadow around my green bloodshot eyes from the wind on the bike.[26]

You're not ready yet, are you?
You need to be alone. Right?

I tossed and turned in bed for hours, fantasizing about what would have happened if I'd let him kiss me.

I got out of bed in the middle of the night and sat at my

---

[26] We stupidly didn't wear helmets as there is no strict law in Greece which enforces such safety measures.

go

skimpy excuse of a desk. Logged into my email. Clicked *Compose*. I stared at the flashing cursor for what seemed like an eternity. Conflicting thoughts raging through my mind like coloured dye in a dish of milk.

My reflection had been nice to me lately. Giving me space to figure out exactly what it was I wanted in my life. A fresh start away from the internal pain? Yes. Some form of happiness? Yes. What would make me happy? I didn't really know yet, but I definitely knew, that as well as writing, I still wanted to play music. I wasn't sure if that would make me happy, but I did know that when I sat down to do something creative, it tamed the negative thoughts. It always had. Ever since that day I'd painted flowers on Demetri's blue Beetle.

With my virtual fingers crossed, and the hope that this wasn't going to ruin my chances of getting back into music, I emailed Serafeim, "I hope we can see each other again ... ."

Drunk on love, once again, I moved half of my stuff into his apartment on the opposite side of the city, and spent multiple nights a week sleeping over.

Three months after that, we rented a new apartment.

Serafeim booked gigs for me at various venues in Athens, encouraging me to flaunt myself as a solo artist. I recorded an EP and sent it out to radio stations and music journalists.[27] He even organized an event I will forever hold dear to my heart: a one-off Hard Candy revival gig with a band from New York called Oneida at The Underworld Club.

Oh, yes. I played guitar on stage with my parents.[28]

But about a year into our relationship, sometime in early to mid 2006, Serafeim asked me, "What are you going to do if we have kids?" He was sitting on a footstool in the middle of our living room, and I was on the couch, feet hooked under my bum, left elbow on the arm rest, holding myself upright.

"What do you mean?" I frowned, flicking hair out of my eyes.

"Would you go on tour and leave them with me?" he said.

"Would that be a problem for you?"

"Yes."

"Why?"

"That's no life," he said. "A life without a mother."

"They wouldn't be without a mother. I would just be doing my job, following my dream."

"You know what it's like growing up like that."

"I was never without my mother."

"But you felt like you were."

Yes. But I didn't anymore. She was healthy again. We were doing fine. And that was different.

I stared into Serafeim's eyes, at his complacent, yet determined expression. I realized, for the first time, the choices my mother had to make. Do you follow an unconventional dream and risk fucking up your kids, or do you give up on your dream to raise your kids in a socially accepted way and risk fucking them up anyway? Because let's face it, people are always going to find excuses to be fucked up.

I snapped out of my trance. "I turned out okay."

"You have scars," he said, as if it was an accusation. But I knew that his abrupt way of speaking was the result of translating from Greek. Greeks don't cushion their words.

"I'm different than her," I said. "I don't need vodka and Valium to play live. I'm not my mother."

Serafeim shook his head.

go

"No. That's the rock 'n' roll life."

"Doesn't *have* to be like that," I said.

"No. But when we have kids, you'll have to quit. I can't be a single dad."

His view on the matter seemed to be final.

And once again, I'd push music to the curb for love.

Even though Serafeim is here, I often feel he is absent. Even when I'm hugging and kissing him, I miss him, as though I am only imagining his touch.

What is loneliness, really? It certainly isn't the result of being alone.

Is it emptiness? Sadness? A yearning for something we don't have; for something we regret letting go?

Is it love that watches the world through a window?

Is it need? Want? Disappointment? Self-loathing?

Does it exist at all?

Does loneliness define us, because we can't define it?

During the winter of 2007, Serafeim and I had been together for about eighteen months. I hadn't yet quit playing gigs, but the prospect of 'having to' meant my reflection pushed and prodded with the temptation to set out on my own. The idea of quitting music began to take its toll.

Stop relying on anyone but yourself.

Serafeim has to go.

Serafeim had done nothing wrong. He'd expressed his opinion. It was not an order. I had the power, like anyone in this world, to make my own decisions. Yet, I still couldn't bring myself to risk losing love over a career. I let him believe that if we had kids, I would quit music.

One night, in a quaint little jazz bar called 56 in Kolonaki, we had a brief irrational argument which escalated. I called him an arsehole for no reason other than being pissed off about him passing judgement about something menial. I can't even remember what it was, but by the time we got home, I was so angry I was ready to leave him.

You don't need a boyfriend.
Would you marry this guy?
Would you have kids with this guy?
What do you see in this guy?
Does he make you happy?
Why does he make you happy?
Do you love him?
Do you really love him?
What do you love about him?
Why do you love those things about him?
You could live without him.
You should be alone.
You've never had time to truly be alone.

The front door ricocheted off the wall as I flung it open, slurring, "Fuck you," navigating the blurry hallway towards the kitchen. This was it. This was the last time I was ever going to have to deal with a motherfucking egocentric Greek who had a problem with ... a problem with what? I'd forgotten what the fight was about, but I knew I couldn't hack it anymore. I couldn't hack being judged, or told how I should be living. I couldn't hack the voice in my head; I couldn't hack the memories of my past behaviour inflicting guilt on me all the time. I shouldn't have had to live like this, constantly struggling with my thoughts and my feelings and self-loathing. I had been doing so well to tame her until ... I got drunk.

go

Leave him.
I should leave you.
It's not me, it's you.
Shut up!
What am I doing?
The right thing.
I'm not! This is not the right thing!
I hate you.
I hate you.
Stop it!
It was final.

I knew I shouldn't have jumped into this relationship so soon. I knew I wasn't ready. I didn't know how to love or be loved. I didn't know how to deal with everyday arguments in a rational and mature way. I'd spent so long running from negative feelings 'inflicted' on me by others. Instead of simply engaging in adult conversation to find a resolution, my instinct was to *abort*.

There was no other sensible choice but to ...
abort abort abort.

Serafeim yelled and screamed obscenities in retaliation to my yelling and screaming of obscenities as I flung my handbag across the room and ripped my black leather jacket off. I don't know where either of them landed, but I tripped over one of them and stumbled. I think I even heard the word 'cunt' probe the beating of my adrenalized heart to go *boom boom boom*, let's get out of this fucking room, house, country even.

Jesus fucking Christ I'm going to throw up.

"You're a fucking arsehole," I screeched.

He said something back. I don't know what. Clearly I disliked it because I grabbed a kitchen chair and dragged it along the marble floor so I could reach the medicine cupboard above the oven fan.

"What the fuck are you doing?" Serafeim said.

Killing myself. I may or may not have uttered it out loud.

I found what I was looking for and jumped off the chair. Serafeim tried to wrestle the packet of Ponstan out of my hands, but I succeeded in retaining them. I bent over the sink with my back to him so he couldn't reach my hands and popped all the pills out of the packaging. They landed in the marble sink, clicking like Tic Tacs hitting concrete.

My hands shook. I was still yelling, slurring my organs through my mouth. His frantic voice incoherently boomed in my ears. He grabbed my shoulder to try and spin me around. I don't know where I got the strength from, but I managed to stay put, and I accidentally punched him in the face.

I scraped up the pills, along with God knows what else that was stuck on the bottom of the sink, and sucked them out of my palm, turned on the tap and shovelled water into my mouth with my hands, constantly flicking my head back to get the damn things down my throat. One or more of the pills got stuck and I gagged.

Swallow.
No.
Swallow.
No.
Swallow!
No!

In this moment of weakness, Serafeim was able to fling me around and he shoved his fingers down my throat, grabbed the back of my head and started shaking it like he was trying to empty a cardboard box.

The room was spinning and I threw up in my mouth,

go

my head pounding with a mixture of traffic, white noise, echoing insults and, once again, self-loathing.

I want to fucking die.

"Did you swallow any?" Serafeim said.

I gulped. I shrugged.

"Did you *fucking* swallow any?"

I stared.

"We're going to the hospital."

"No."

"Tell me you didn't swallow any."

"I didn't swallow any."

I may have. I couldn't tell. My whole body felt like it'd been shoved through a drain cleaner.

We stared at each other for a moment, catching our breaths. Serafeim hugged me, took me into the bathroom and forced me to throw up. I did.

We went to bed in silence. He tried to speak to me, but I ignored him and turned my back, facing the bookcase. I wasn't worried about dying in my sleep.

I stared at a blurry title of some novel, *The Girls' Guide to ...*

I closed my eyes and finished it off in my head: *Death.*

The next morning, I looked at myself in the bathroom mirror with complete and utter disgust.

Where the fuck do I go from here?

Can you forgive me for all the times I've looked at you and seen a face and head attached to a body with arms and legs? I was mistaken to think it was me I was looking at. I realize now that I am not you. I know we spend a lot of time together. Especially in the morning, when I brush my teeth and wonder when you'll start to lose them. And

in those evenings when I force myself to go out and 'have a good time.' Sometimes I make you look pretty. Other times I can't make you look pretty no matter how hard I try. But that's the thing. Is there any point in making you look pretty when you're just a reflection of a face and body?

You keep showing me that thirty-five-year-old face and body as if it's inadequate, and keep asking me what happened to the eighteen-year-old model-like physique you used to have, which you also made me loathe. So what? You're ten kilos heavier. Why does it even matter anyway? We are not the same. The weight is weightless on you. You are just a reflection.

If I really didn't care, I'd become a recluse, and really get fat, old, and ugly and not give a shit. But I do still have some pride. Thank goodness, because if I didn't I'd be living in shadows.

And I'm proud I've been able to stop concerning myself with how others perceive me, so stop looking back at me through the mirror with judgement smeared all over your skin and through your hair. Stop blowing the taste of unacceptance into my first morning breath.

I will just breathe it out again.

Your judgement makes me want to turn heads. But that's not who I am anymore. I don't want people looking at me because I am weird and mysterious and dress strangely. I want people to look at me when I start talking because they're interested in what I have to say.

I want conversation, not admiration.

I can't take you out of the mirror. I can only keep a record of what you look like. I see you, but I can never feel you. Most of the time, I don't understand how we are connected. Our features, sure, they're similar, but not always identical.

go

I'm sorry I have treated you based on a misconception.

Do you feel what I feel? Do you notice that when I'm putting lipstick on, and then smile at you, that I'm thinking, "What's the fucking point?" It hurts me when I feel that way. I would like it to stop. I think it might be you putting that thought in my head.

Have you considered what it's like when other people mistake you for me? I've learnt how to speak and move like you, you know. It's probably because I've been a bit slack in dressing you up like I did when I was into music more than writing. It's hard to find any reason to. All you do is project a feeling of inadequacy over me.

So I ignore you.

Often.

I'm sorry.

I'm just going to say it ...

I think you should move out.

Thirty-five years is a long time to be with someone you don't often get along with, don't you think? It's not me, it's you. Ha! No, really. It is. You need to stop reaching into my brain when I look at you, and I need to stop thinking that you and I are the same.

We are not the same.

You are my reflection.

It's time now.

It's time ... for you to 'Go.'

In late 2007, Serafeim and I took a long weekend to escape the rat race and spent it in Zachlorou, a lush green village built on a mountain slope on the left bank of the river Vouraikos which forms a narrow gorge.

We slept, we ate, we talked about our dreams.

Having forced myself to accept the prospect of quitting

music without first trying to discuss with Serafeim how it made me feel, I told him I wanted to be able to quit New Editions, and go freelance, so I could find more time to write my novel. He said it would be really hard, but that he'd support me.

This acceptance from him warmed my heart.

He suggested I try and acquire some freelance jobs on the side while staying in full-time employment to get my foot in the door.

The connections I'd made at New Editions allowed me to do this.

And then I soon quit ... to open a gourmet sandwich bar, called Isalos, with Serafeim on Ithaca. It was Serafeim's idea. Why did I continue to walk myself in directions that did not seem to be on my own map?

Isalos was the biggest business mistake of my life, but it was also an emotionally enlightening mistake. I was plunged into an environment I severely disliked (I'd had my fair share of hospitality jobs in my lifetime, and I still hadn't gotten over the bad taste Ithaca had left in my mouth from Hector), yet managed to make the shop work, *and* be a financial success, in only three months.

Serafeim knew nothing about the industry, and therefore left all the decisions and organization up to me. This was a massive strain on our relationship, because I expected us to be equals, for us to do it together, to see if we could live the Greek island dream (work six months, not work six months, which I could dedicate to writing), but I essentially became his 'boss.' That was not an ideal way to venture into the second year of a relationship, especially considering my tendency to shut myself off in times of struggle.

But.

Because I was forced to stick something out that was

extraordinarily challenging, both physically and emotionally, and I had a lot of time to be alone in my head, I learnt a few things that helped me cope with my erratic emotional stability and depression.

This was the time 'alone' I needed to figure a few things out.

I discovered, after a huge argument with Serafeim over the disparity of our 'shared' responsibilities that would have typically made me flee, that people can still love each other when times are tough.

I discovered that every time I thought I was no longer loved, I was mistaken. The feeling of being unloved and unwanted was a projection of my past. I didn't need to let go of it, but I needed to accept it, and understand that it is all a part of what makes me who I am today.

I discovered, that in order to love myself, I had to understand *her*, the cold hard side of my personality that prefers to run than face reality. I learnt to respect her behaviour, even when it seemed like it was the wrong way to be. And that doesn't mean I am a bad person; it means I cope the only way I know how.

I discovered that I can create my own freedom. There is no such thing as obtaining it. Freedom is everywhere I look if I choose to see it as a choice. And there is never a wrong choice if I embrace the lessons I learn along the way, even when they seem like they will be the death of me.

I discovered that happiness isn't something I will always feel, even when I think I should—simply because I am a lucky person. Happiness is not a state of being, it's a perspective, and just like freedom, that too is a choice. Happiness also comes in many forms, it ebbs and flows, it's sometimes overwhelming, it's sometimes faint, and it sometimes disappears completely. But it's always attainable if I look around the corner.

I discovered that yes, if there is a will, there *is* a way, but that not everyone is strong enough to find their way, or even have the will, and I should be proud of myself, because I have found both. Even for the simplest of things, like acknowledging this very fact.

I discovered that yes, *she* was right: we *are* alone in this world. And that is not something to be depressed about. It is something to rejoice. Loneliness inspires me. Loneliness writes my books and music. Loneliness is my fortune, my ticket to another day. It's also my happiness. Happiness is a strange emotion. It doesn't always do what it says on the box.

Isalos did not, however, only gift me with a new perspective on life. It gifted me with Holly Bolly. Holly Bolly is a female Dalmatian who Serafeim and I adopted in May of 2007 when we were running the café-bar. She was only thirty days old. As of writing this, she is almost ten. The saying that a dog is a man's best friend should not cause people's eyes to roll. Because she is often the only living being that makes me smile when all I want to do is cry. Holly has also taught me many things, but the most important thing is this: If you get a good balance of food, play time, and love, nothing else really matters.

Isalos lasted for one summer. We hated it. But at least we can say we gave it our best shot. Now the romantic notion of running a bar on a Greek island is no longer a tempting 'what if,' it's a 'been there done that, don't ever think about it again.'

In 2008, I scored a part-time job at Macmillan Education. I earned more working part-time at Macmillan than I did working full time at New Editions, and I finally had some spare time to write what was one day to become my debut novel, *String Bridge*.²⁹ It was a step forward. It boosted my confidence, and I knew, deep down, that *that* wasn't luck. That was hard work. I worked *hard* to be qualified for that job.

I had also now written some material in a couple of course books for New Editions, so I had reached the goal of seeing myself in print. But I desperately wanted a *novel* in print. English language teaching material wasn't the dream; it was only a stepping stone.

If there is a will there is a way.

I have to remind myself every day, that I am lucky.

Happiness is not a state of being, it's a perspective. And it doesn't always do what it says on the box.

Freedom is always going to be a mind over matter deal.

Yes. Yes. Yes.

But ...

Sometimes I sit on the couch with Serafeim in the evening and say nothing. And Serafeim says nothing. Sometimes we can go for days and days saying nothing to each other on the couch. Some may feel that such silence would mean a relationship is on its way out. That there is no spark, no excitement, that something needs to be done about it before it fizzles and dies.

Sometimes, I do feel like that.

But other times, I don't.

I don't because all it takes is one of Serafeim's melancholy glances, fleeting smiles, and impromptu winks for the silence we share to be rich with our voices.

I see myself in him sometimes.

I see the persistent battle with hopelessness in his eyes—something I believe all creative people possess. I also see that without each other, that battle would be harder to fight, unbearable even. And even when I'm having one of those moments of wanting to flee, deep down I know I am just having a knee-jerk reaction to the fear of failure and self-acceptance.

Because during those nights on the couch, we understand each other when no words are spoken.

Unuttered words—always—mean so much more. They speak the deepest truths, the ones we can never hide—even from ourselves—and are forced to confront on a daily basis. And when I catch that wink, that melancholy glance, I know we have communicated on a level neither of us will ever truly understand in this lifetime.

And I think that's enough. No ... I know that's enough. To have a true soul mate, a best friend, doesn't mean eternal bliss. It means you have someone who is not going to run when times get tough, and who is going to understand even when they disagree.

Serafeim is the only person I can sit in the same room with for twenty-four hours without saying a word, without wondering if I've done something wrong.

Because sometimes words aren't necessary to say, "I love you."

Even though they were few and far between, 2008 was the year I played my last solo gig. I was the support act for Holly Golightly and the Brokeoffs at Club Rodeo in Athens. The review on mic.gr of my performance was dire: "... Jessica Bell, for about thirty minutes, expressed her singer-songwriter woes and I doubt if anyone even remembers anything from them." I wasn't surprised. I hated playing solo. All the attention on me and nothing but me, made me feel trapped in the expectations of others. I wanted to play music, but I needed a *band*.

go

Though kids were still not on the horizon for me and Serafeim, I stopped trying to push my music career after that. It seemed useless. What milestones would I ever reach in a country like Greece? And seeing as I would eventually have to quit to start a family, it seemed better to quit now before I (as unlikely as it seemed) made anything of myself.

But I struggled with my decision. A lot. And *still*, after three years of being with Serafeim, I felt that long-standing need to be accepted and loved, and if quitting music to have kids was what I thought I needed to do for Serafeim to accept and love me, then I had to do it. For reasons I still don't understand today, I held onto that conversation, even though the topic had not ever been revived.

I like to believe I didn't change who I was for Serafeim, but rather channelled my creative energy elsewhere: into writing.

Despite his influence, I owned that choice. But I can't help holding it against him, and the regret often extracts itself—bit by bit—through meaningless bickering. I know I could have held my ground that day back in 2006, and said, "I'm not giving up music. You can love me or leave me." But I didn't. I was scared. I wanted to spend the rest of my life with him. And I hadn't yet grown up enough to realize, if he truly loved me, he would accept that.

So I convinced myself that writing was the be-all and end-all. That being a writer was my true calling. My mum, on the other hand, didn't stop bugging me to write more music and play gigs again.

"It's a waste of talent," she'd say. "You're brilliant at it, Juice. You're flushing a gift down the toilet."

Mum's words convinced me even more that I'd made

the right decision by giving up music. The choice had now doubled as another form of rebellion, which tricked me into thinking I was acting independently.

For the last ten years, I've honestly believed I'd made the right decision. Let me rephrase that ... it wasn't a *wrong* decision, it was just not the *quintessential* decision.

Of course there have been ups and downs, but I have been 'happy' in general. My writing and publishing career has flourished so much now that it is how I make a living. But the day I finished writing the first draft of this memoir in early 2016, I realized that there was still a big gaping hole in my heart.

There was no resolution to this story. I couldn't find a way to give this memoir, and my readers, an element of closure, and resigned myself to the fact that it would remain open-ended. Because making a living off writing and publishing was not a satisfying ending to me.

I started to think about all the years I had spent immersing myself in song, and why—in the deepest depths of my psyche—is the *real* reason I quit music? Was I running again? And if so, from what exactly?

I know that initially I had sought a career in music because that's what everyone, especially my mother, kept encouraging me to do. Was I just following in my parents' footsteps, or following my own dream? I wanted so much to follow my own dream. A dream that was wholly *mine*. So I let my past trick me into thinking I needed to be completely removed from it to find it.

My talent for making music came so naturally that I had taken it for granted.

But what hadn't come naturally with music was *weightlessness*. What hadn't come naturally with music was the sense of freedom that writing offered me.

go

I grasped for this sense of freedom every chance I got. Because that freedom, was also freedom from myself.

After experiencing this freedom, I began to believe that music weakened me—made me a slave to my reflection. My heart would bind to every note, like strings are bound to a guitar. And every once in a while, those strings would go out of tune, and they'd need winding, up and down, up and down, until the tuning was once again even. Because if the strings aren't tuned to perfection, the music they make is either too flat, or too sharp. There is no stability in an out-of-tune guitar. And if my heart loses balance when it's bound to those strings, so does my mind.

So instead of playing gigs, I used music to fuel my writing. As time went by, I discovered I was more easily able to express my feelings that way. The problem was, those feelings were no longer mine. They were those of the characters in my books.

This was still not a healthy solution. I was still running—escaping from emotional conflict by transferring them to fictional beings.

Is anything about me real at all?

The day I sent the first draft of this memoir to my editor, I thought I would feel a huge sense of relief that I had finally got everything off my chest.

But I didn't. Not at all.

Because what I really needed to get off my chest was that I've been lying to myself my entire life.

My reflection has not been out to get me. She has not been pushing me to get in touch with my evil side. All she's been doing is pushing me to admit—and accept—the truth about myself.

I'm allowed to challenge the opinions of others to better myself.

I do not need third party validation.

I can just be a person, like everyone else, who seizes opportunities.

They are simply choices.

Choices *I* can make. No harm is going to come from making my own choices.

What's stopping me from doing music alongside writing books?

Being in the spotlight: me and my guitar up for scrutiny.

So why don't you start a band?

Because I have enough responsibilities in my life. I don't want to have to bleed and sweat for the success of yet another new project that will be suppressed by circumstance.

But you miss music.

Should I start a band?

Yes, you should start a band.

What will Serafeim think?

You've been together for ten years, do you really think he's going to leave you because you decide to do something that you love?

No. But starting a band scares me.

Then at least start song writing again, think about producing a new album and releasing it independently. It doesn't matter if it sells or makes money, right? All you want is to sing again?

Yes, sing. I don't care for the guitar. It has always been a means to write songs and sing. I just want to sing.

Then what's stopping you?

The next day, a miracle happened.

I received a very unexpected email from George, the guy who runs Artracks Recording Studios near where I live. I thought it was going to be about another voiceover job. Until I read the subject line: *Jessica ... in a band?*

I sucked in my breath and clicked on the email.

```
Hi Jessica!
I hope all is fine! I was just wondering ... I
have a good friend who has a very successful
band and are looking for a female singer. They
have done some albums and a lot of touring and
there's more to come. They toured the US at
least two times (last year for something like
fifty gigs—from medium-sized clubs to big festi-
vals) and have played in most European cities
as well. Whenever they play in Athens it's
usually sold out.

The name of the band is Keep Shelly in Athens.
They are looking for a good female singer (pref-
erably native English speaking) who will be
available for tours (whenever they are arranged)
and live dates and some studio recording.

I don't know if all that fits your schedule of
course, but I thought I'd ask since this is
maybe the most successful Greek band abroad as
we speak. You can Google / YouTube them to see
what it's all about if you like.

Let me know what you think.

All the best!
```

I couldn't believe it. Did I have a fairy god mother I didn't know about? Is this what they call pure alignment of the stars?

I went for an audition. They chose me out of seven other candidates.

I accepted the offer.

I made the decision without consulting Serafeim. Instead, I announced my decision and asked him to be happy for me.

"I am happy for you. But things are going to change, you know that, right?" Serafeim said.

"In what way?"

"You know ... Drugs, sex, rock 'n' roll."

I laughed and said, "How old do you think I am?"

Serafeim shrugged. "It'll be hard to get used to."

"Don't worry. I'll always be the same Jessica." A few tears slid down my cheeks, overwhelmed by what I had just done. "Do you still love me?" I asked.

"Of course. You are my creature," he said. "And you're beautiful when you cry."

After performing for the first time with Keep Shelly in Athens in Crete in late 2016, it hit me: I don't need to rebel against the world as a means to escape myself.

Because I don't need to run anymore.

I like being me. Just another human being. In this world. Writing and singing.

Making tomorrow worth breathing for.

acknowledgements

First and foremost I must thank my parents for giving me their blessing to publish this book. It was extremely hard to write this memoir honestly without airing some of their dirty laundry too. There are some things they remember differently and/or don't remember at all. Memory is a funny thing. It really is different for everyone. So thank you Mum and Demetri, from the bottom of my heart, for your acceptance, encouragement, and support in writing this book on my own terms.

A huge thank you also goes out to Jenny Heath, who not only read an early draft of this book, but has been a devoted friend since 2005. We always laugh about the fact that she hardly (if ever) sees the dark and depressed side of my personality. That's because when I'm around her, my happy side is dominant. Thank you, Jenny, for always bringing out the best in me.

Thank you to Karen Fisher, who helped to clarify a few details about our high school life. The character named Kerry in this memoir is based on three fabulous ladies who inspired me to reach for the stars in my late teen years and early adulthood. Karen is one of those ladies. The other two are Caitlin Griffith and Sally Reiffel. Thank you for helping me escape the horrible rut of depression on many an occasion.

Thank you, also, to all the writing and publishing professionals who helped make this book what it is: Roz Morris for doing a development edit on the first draft, and

Dan Holloway for doing a development edit on the second draft. Glynis Smy and Dawn Ius for beta reading the first draft. Jane Davis, Peter Snell, and Alison Ripley-Cubitt for beta reading the second draft. Orna Ross, founder of The Alliance of Independent Authors for her legal advice. And Amie McCracken for proofing and formatting. Thank you also to all you fabulous fans who follow me on social media. Your encouragement during the production of this book has been inconceivable.

links of interest

If you'd like to see a gallery of photographs from Jessica's past, go to:

bit.ly/DearReflectionPhotoGallery

For all Jessica's music links go to:

bit.ly/JessicaBellsMusic

If you'd like to discover more about Erika Bach and Demetri Vlass, check out these links:

bit.ly/HardCandyAU
bit.ly/HardCandyYouTube
bit.ly/ErikaBachSolo
bit.ly/DemetriVlassSolo
bit.ly/ApeTheCryYouTube

If you'd like to discover more about Keep Shelly in Athens, check out these links:

bit.ly/KeepShelly_InAthens
bit.ly/KeepShellyYouTube
bit.ly/KeepShellySpotify
bit.ly/KeepShellyiTunes
bit.ly/KeepShellyFacebook
bit.ly/KeepShellyTwitter
bit.ly/KeepShellyInstagram

a letter from erika bach

Dear Readers,

When I first suffered from Benzodiazepine and other physician prescribed medication withdrawal, there was no information online or elsewhere on the symptoms or the dangers, or the possibilities of protracted, debilitating illnesses (iatrogenic illnesses) that many medications inflict on an unknowing public who believes the medical profession would do no harm. I do believe that doctors believe they do no harm, but with the pharmaceutical companies being their only means of knowing about medications and their effects, it makes for a dangerous cocktail of misinformation for the patient.

The illness syndromes brought about by medications are insidious and difficult to pinpoint as the cause, but with so many syndromes that have no medical test affirmations of being physical, other than severe pain syndromes, not to mention debilitating depression and anxiety which then gives birth to rage or catatonia, I looked closer at what I was ingesting to find the cause of my severe and long lasting problems.

I had every test known to man, all coming back clear. I was looked on as a hypochondriac or someone in need of emotional help. I was neither. My body had slowly been poisoned over many years and decided enough was enough by giving me a complete and total breakdown. Physically and mentally. For over a year I had to learn to walk, eat, sit, move from room to room, bend my body, not be freaked out by air moving around me. I had waking hallucinations, severe pain from head to toe; I was in a state of high panic. I could hear the grass grow and the blood pump through my veins. I didn't sleep for more than a few minutes at a time for an entire year. I was rigid and my skin was hypersensitive. It felt like there were shards of glass just under the surface. Excruciating pain each time I moved.

There were hundreds more symptoms. They came and went, sometimes quickly, sometimes not. It ruined my life and those I loved, and despite being left to deal with it on my own, I completely understand their frustration and anger. I acted and looked crazy. There was no reason for them to believe what I was going through was real. I couldn't believe it myself until I happened upon Tranx, an organization in Melbourne Australia who helped people get off Benzos in particular. They were my saviours. Although they couldn't take the pain from me, or the anxiety, they gave me and my family the knowledge that what I had would eventually pass. I was not crazy. I had an iatrogenic illness. Protracted withdrawal syndrome.

If you have symptoms your doctor can't get to the bottom of, I suggest you look at the medications you have taken, not just recently, but back for some years. For instance, Cipro, a popular antibiotic, has devastating long term complications, yet few people know about it, instead heading back to the doctors for more medications which then only complicate the syndrome further.

You will find many helpful sites online by using search terms such as iatrogenesis, benzodiazepine withdrawal symptoms, Cipro side effects/withdrawal. You may or may not be surprised that ALL medications will have an effect on you, and over a lifetime of taking poison into your system, it's not so far-fetched that you will be affected by it most severely in your middle to old age, during the time you need your health the most.

I used myself as a guinea pig. Once I believed the cause of my illnesses, I stopped taking all drugs, no matter how bad it got. I took nothing. Over a seven-year period my symptoms either decreased or disappeared, leaving me with quite a normal life. A life I would not have had, had I listened to the doctors instead of my gut. Being poisoned has left me compromised. I have many allergies to chemicals, preservatives, alcohol, chocolate, or caffeine. I don't get rashes, I get central nervous system symptoms. My life can still be turned upside down without notice, but now I know the cause, it's made it much easier to get through. Easier for me and for those I love.

While I was on medications, I constantly had back problems. Since not taking drugs, I have no back problem.

While I was on medications I always suffered from migraines. Since stopping, I get no migraines.

While on medication, I became physically rigid. Since stopping, I'm as agile as I was when I was teenager.

When I was on medication I would get upset too easily, have rages, depression, and panic attacks. Since stopping, I have none of those things. My chemical sensitivities can bring about anxious feelings and depression, along with some milder physical pains, but all are manageable now and have little impact on my life.

My road to recovery is far from over because unfortunately Cipro has some lasting effects that change your body's DNA. I can also get a little scared about hurting myself as my choices are to become a vegetable were I to take medications again, or to suffer in pain. I try not to think about it and just get on with my life. It's much happier and fuller since the reasons for my unexplainable illnesses were finally explained and I could get on with recovering from being poisoned.

I'm not trying to convince you to never take medicine. All I'm saying is, please, for yourself and for your loved ones, do your research, don't be afraid to challenge your doctor, and before ingesting anything, ask yourself, "Is it a Band-Aid or a cure?" If it's a Band-Aid, chances are you'll be better off without it.

Erika

Enjoyed this book?
Go to *jessicabellauthor.com*
to find more.

To sign up to Jessica's newsletter
and/or connect with her
on social media go to
iamjessicabell.com.

Are you a writer?
You might be interested in Jessica's
Writing in a Nutshell series.

Lightning Source UK Ltd.
Milton Keynes UK
UKHW040738030321
379707UK00001B/33